Deleuze

Charlie Jans 10/15
(Bristol)

Key Contemporary Thinkers

Published

Deleuze

Reidar Due

polity

The right of Reidar Due to be identified as Author of this Work has been asserted in accordance with the UK Copyright, Designs and Patents Act 1988.

First published in 2007 by Polity Press

Polity Press
65 Bridge Street
Cambridge CB2 1UR, UK

Polity Press
350 Main Street
Malden, MA 02148, USA

ISBN-10: 0-7456-3034-0
ISBN-13: 978-07456-3034-2
ISBN-10: 0-7456-3035-9 (pb)
ISBN-13: 978-07456-3035-9 (pb)

A catalogue record for this book is available from the British Library.

Typeset in $10\frac{1}{2}$ on 12 pt Palatino
by SNP Best-set Typesetter Ltd, Hong Kong
Printed and bound in Great Britain by MPG Books Ltd, Bodmin, Cornwall

The publisher has used its best endeavours to ensure that the URLs for external websites referred to in this book are correct and active at the time of going to press. However, the publisher has no responsibility for the websites and can make no guarantee that a site will remain live or that the content is or will remain appropriate.

Every effort has been made to trace all copyright holders, but if any have been inadvertently overlooked the publishers will be pleased to include any necessary credits in any subsequent reprint or edition.

For further information on Polity, visit our website: www.polity.co.uk

Contents

Acknowledgements

This book started its life in the congenial intellectual environment of Wadham College, Oxford. It was completed under the equally excellent working conditions of Magdalen College, Oxford. Prashant Kidambi, Rochana Bajpai and two anonymous readers for Polity read the text and made helpful comments.

Introduction

The Philosophy of Gilles Deleuze

This book is an introduction to the philosophy of Gilles Deleuze (1925–95). It presents his philosophy both as a philosophical system and as a critical enterprise. The system contains a philosophy of the mind and its place in reality. This philosophy of mind is applied within various domains of social reality and epistemology, giving rise to a series of original theories of language, sexuality, art, politics, history and science. The critical enterprise lends force to this system and its applications. The philosophy of Deleuze questions some of our most deeply entrenched and widely shared beliefs about thought, experience and reality. One can say about Deleuze's philosophy what is often said about French surrealism, namely, that it aims to produce a *revolution* in the mind, a fundamental change in how we think. This book presents the development of Deleuze's system and the implications of his critical project in the spheres of political theory, ethics, aesthetics and the epistemology of the human sciences.

Deleuze seeks to replace the practical and rational view of reality that we derive from everyday experience with a philosophical speculative account of reality. A central feature of this new account is that the human being is not presented as a conscious centre of action and belief. In the philosophical tradition the concept of the 'subject' grants precisely such a privileged role to the human being and to self-conscious thought. Deleuze's philosophy is therefore also a critique of the concept of the subject. This critique is not a straightforward attack or rejection; his philosophy constructs different and quite sophisticated arguments to show that what the philosophy of the subject takes as an origin or a basic premise (self-consciousness, individual freedom) is in fact derived from or produced within a larger process bearing no resemblance to subjective experience. In Deleuze's account of reality, the human being occupies a limited place as a process unfolding amidst other processes to which it is subordinated and with which it interacts.

Central to this new conception of reality is a philosophy of signs and signification, or 'semiotics'. Signification is here neither a mental occurrence, nor a social convention. Nor is signification a material thing. It is thus neither mental, material nor social. Signification has its own unique place in reality, its own 'ontological status'. Deleuze argues that from the point of view of this special ontological status of signification we can gain a very different conception as well of the psyche, of political power, of social and cultural practices. The application of 'semiotics' to a general theory of the mind, politics and culture is the joint project of Deleuze and his collaborator, the psychiatrist and political activist, Félix Guattari (1930–92).

The principal aim of the present book is to understand how Deleuze develops a metaphysics and a semiotics in his early work and how he then with Guattari applies these metaphysical and semiotic principles within the sphere of a general and formal social theory.

Deleuze's work can be divided into three separate stages. During the first period, from the early 1950s to around 1970, Deleuze established himself as a French academic philosopher, first, as a historian of philosophy, then as an important independent philosopher, with the two parallel treatises: *Difference and Repetition* (1968) and *The Logic of Sense* (1969). During this period, Deleuze developed original theories of time, language, signs, and the relationship between thought and reality.

In the second period from 1970 to the early 1980s, Deleuze entered an intensive working relationship with Félix Guattari. Together they wrote two influential works in social and political theory under the common title *Capitalism and Schizophrenia*. The first was entitled *Anti-Oedipus* (1972) and consisted of a critical discussion of psychoanalysis and an original reinterpretation of Marxist social theory.

The second volume was called *A Thousand Plateaus* (1980) and covered a much wider range of topics, arising mostly from a critique of the contemporary social and human sciences. These topics all involve the central questions of the early work concerning significa- tion and the relationship between thought and reality.

As a bridge between these two books, they wrote an essay on the writer Franz Kafka: *Kafka: Toward a Minor Literature* (1975). During this period Deleuze also became well known as a professor of phi- losophy at the newly opened university at Vincennes outside Paris and took on the role of a public intellectual. He and his contempo- rary Michel Foucault were perceived as the representatives of a new 'Nietzschean' philosophy, a philosophy that would adhere to none of the other philosophical currents at the time, whether Marxist, psychoanalytical or phenomenological.

During the last stage of his life, from 1980 to 1995, Deleuze's collaboration with Guattari became less central to his work. He wrote a series of books on art and the craft of philosophy, includ- ing an essay on Leibniz and baroque art and a study of the late twentieth-century British painter, Francis Bacon. The book, *What Is Philosophy?*, was nominally co-authored with Guattari. These texts are all concerned with the question of how art and philosophy are parallel, yet distinct, practices of thought and creation.

Here we follow the chronological development of Deleuze's phi- losophy. Chapter 1 is devoted to Deleuze's early thought; Chapters 2–4 concentrate on the common philosophical enterprise of Deleuze and Guattari, while the final chapter discusses Deleuze's theory of philosophy and art and the potential ethical implications of his philosophy as a whole. The book thus presents an account of Deleuze's intellectual development with a marked focus on the middle period.

The discussion of this development is held together by a problem regarding philosophical method: how does Deleuze think? What are the strategies of thought, principles and methods that orient his thinking and its relation to other systems of thought?

The early work proposes, that is, theorizes as well as demon- strates, a genetic method in accordance with a principle of 'imma- nence'. The collaborative work starts from this genetic method, but seeks to combine it with materialist premises about the relationship between the psyche and society. Deleuze and Guattari develop the genetic method in a different, less formal and less cosmological direction. It is now not a question of understanding how the mind is engendered within a cosmic reality, but how the unconscious mind, the psyche that processes sexual desire, is shaped by its place within social and political reality.

In conducting this argument, Deleuze and Guattari encounter a problem concerning *history*, a problem which I believe is decisive in their thinking and accounts for much of its force and originality. Inspired by Nietzsche's genealogical philosophy of history, Deleuze and Guattari in *Anti-Oedipus* develop their own genealogical account of how the psyche comes to form part of the body politic. *A Thousand Plateaus* refines and complicates this method. The structure of the argument put forward in the present book is dictated by this move in their thought from a genetic to a genealogical method.

Thematically, the book traces the problem of the subject throughout Deleuze's work. The early historical works present a critique of the Cartesian and Kantian subject of consciousness and proposes an alternative philosophy of mental activity considered as *affect*, *memory* and the expression of *forces*. *Anti-Oedipus* and *A Thousand Plateaus* each present a historical and semiotic account of the subject as a certain kind of cultural and social *construct*. This culturally or socially constructed subject is then contrasted with marginal subject positions, the schizophrenic and the nomad, and more generally the subject of 'becoming', a subject that escapes social integration as it is defined in terms of its own desires and passage through time.

There are a number of different contexts in which we can situate Deleuze's work. We can group these into three categories: (1) dominant positions within the philosophical tradition that Deleuze engages with, either appropriatively or critically; (2) the theories and methods employed in the human and social sciences, such as Marxism, psychoanalysis or structural linguistics; and, finally, (3) the scholarly literature on Deleuze.

In this book I first situate Deleuze within the philosophical tradition in order to explain the speculative and critical direction of his philosophy. In the sections on *Anti-Oedipus*, *Kafka: Toward a Minor Literature*, and *A Thousand Plateaus*, the book presents Deleuze and Guattari's discussions of psychoanalysis, Marxism and structuralist theories of meaning from the point of view of the new social and 'semiotic' theory that they seek to develop.

As for the scholarly literature, it is very interesting partly because of the lack of agreement among scholars about the nature and direction of Deleuze's thought. The literature has thus identified a number of ambiguous points in Deleuze's philosophy largely having to do with the relationship between its general conception of reality and the mind and its possible practical applications. This book takes a middle course in relation to these issues: Deleuze's philosophy is neither so abstract as to be divorced from practical relevance nor is it in any way directly 'applicable' to experience, in the manner, say, of a scientific theory.

Deleuze's early philosophy develops out of a critical engagement with large parts of the philosophical tradition. His own early philosophy concerns how mental activity is situated within reality. The area of the philosophical tradition that has had the strongest influence on Deleuze's work is thus a group of philosophers who have addressed this question. The philosophers that Deleuze makes his main interlocutors further share a common perspective on this problem. They consider the mind to be an activity that unfolds within a larger set of forces or energies that constitute the cosmos or the world as a whole. The crucial feature of this picture of the mind is that mental activity is seen to be part of the world and not separate from it: the mind is not a screen. Mental activity does not consist in producing a 'representation' of something outside of itself. It is an activity that unfolds in response to forces around it. The philosophers Deleuze enlists as holding such views are the Stoics, Spinoza, Leibniz, Nietzsche and Bergson.[1]

Deleuze in his early work develops a general theory of signification or 'sense'. In the texts written with Guattari this theory of sense is fused with a political and social theory of desire and the psyche. According to this new theory, psychic processes and sexual desire are not simply located in individuals but form an integral part of social and political reality. This perspective on the psyche also leads to a critical discussion of *psychoanalysis*, and in particular the version of psychoanalysis presented by Jacques Lacan (who had been Guattari's analyst). The psyche, according to Lacan, relates to the world and to itself primarily through the medium of *language*. *Anti-Oedipus* presents a semiotic theory that is meant to constitute an alternative to this Lacanian theory of linguistic mediation.

On the basis of this, first, semiotic theory presented through a discussion of psychoanalysis, Deleuze and Guattari, in their subsequent works *Kafka: Toward a Minor Literature* and *A Thousand Plateaus*, present a general semiotic theory of mental activity and cultural practices. This theory, which is embedded in an equally general account of social reality, has the ambitious aim of overturning an entrenched system of thought. This is a cognitive and semiotic system that is embedded in social practices, conforms to everyday experience and has been dominant within large sections of the philosophical tradition (Aristotle, Descartes, Kant). Deleuze in his early work calls this cognitive system 'representation'.

The continuity between the early work and the collaborative work consists, on the one hand, of a critique of this system of representation, and, on the other, of a programme for philosophy which Deleuze calls 'immanence'. The terms 'representation' and 'immanence' are mutually exclusive and define each other: representation consists of thinking about the world through the filter of a logical model centred on the notion of the 'individual object', and corresponding thereby to how the world presents itself in everyday experience. Immanence is the ideal of understanding reality, not as it appears in experience, but as it unfolds according to its own intrinsic genetic processes.

The continuity of aim and method between the historical and metaphysical work of Deleuze in the 1960s and the social and semiotic theory developed in common by Deleuze and Guattari during the 1970s still leaves open a range of interpretative questions concerning Deleuze's work: is his philosophy primarily a metaphysics which only accidentally is applied – or applicable – to social themes, or is it, on the other hand, primarily a social theory relying, accidentally, on some more general underlying principles?

In the critical literature on Deleuze, there is widespread disagreement about how to answer this question, and thus about the fundamental nature of his philosophy, its purpose and central concerns. This means, for instance, that scholars disagree about the relationship between ontology – the philosophy of being – and epistemology – the philosophy of how the mind relates to reality. Are the theory of the mind in *Difference and Repetition* and the discussion of the human sciences in *A Thousand Plateaus* ontological in nature? Do they mainly concern how, at a very abstract level, we ought to think about anything in reality? Or can we derive from these discussions something resembling a method for the human or the social sciences?

Most commentators disagree sharply on the further issue: is Deleuze a political philosopher? Some say that he is, that his philosophy is conducive to certain kinds of political analysis and action, whereas others deny this, claiming that his ontology is such that it rules out any such consequences for action. One can bring the two perspectives together as Dorothea Olkowski does:

> In other words, a theory of change demands concepts that are made from real change and that make change real. And, I will argue, it is only by conceiving life, including duration and subjectivity, in the

image of flows that such a conception of change in the subject and the cosmos can come to be realized.[2]

Olkowski here argues that Deleuze's ontology of time and change is the foundation for a political theory of action, but other commentators, notably in the French tradition (Badiou, Bergen, Zoubarchivili), have tended to emphasize the formal and abstract character of Deleuze's ontology over its practical implications, to the point, in the case of Badiou, of ruling out that Deleuze's thought can have any concrete implications for politics.

A related area of disagreement is linked to the new perspective on the world entailed by Deleuze's ontology. Seeking to displace the consciously thinking and acting human being from the centre of its own life and experience, to present the human being as an interplay of forces taking place within a larger play of forces, Deleuze's philosophy raises the question: what about the human *subject*, the *I* that thinks and feels and chooses?

These three areas of discussion, (1) ontology vs epistemology, (2) ontology vs politics and (3) ontology vs subjectivity, are linked. The question is to what extent Deleuze's philosophy of being is presented from a point of view so distant from human affairs and endeavours as to have no consequences for our actions and for our involvement in political and scientific problems.

The Programme

According to the reading presented in this book, the central principle of Deleuze's philosophy is 'immanence'. Conventionally, 'immanence' is a metaphysical concept opposed to 'transcendence'. It characterizes the theology and cosmology of Spinoza's philosophy of 'divine nature'. In Spinoza's system, there is no God outside of reality, 'transcending' nature. The only God there is for Spinoza is a principle of creation that is inherent to, immanent within, divine nature. Deleuze has written a study of Spinoza's principle of immanence, *Spinoza and the Problem of Expression* (1968).[3] He there interprets the principle of immanence in Spinoza with the aid of the concept of 'expression', taken from Leibniz. The immanence of God in nature and of all finite, created beings in God means for Spinoza, according to Deleuze, that divine nature expresses itself in all things. This expressive relationship entails a particular notion of causality: the expressive principle is cause of the finite being that it expresses itself through, but this cause is nowhere visible within experience in the manner of physical causes. The expressive cause is an internal or 'genetic' principle.

It is this notion of an internal genetic cause that Deleuze takes from Spinoza and which becomes the impetus for his own philosophy. By extending the use of this genetic principle from its original, theological, context, Deleuze also extends the meaning of the concept of 'immanence'. This concept becomes for Deleuze a principle of thought rather than a property of reality. The principle of immanence means, positively, to think genetically, i.e. to reproduce in thought the genetic process that engendered an object. Negatively, immanence is defined in opposition to those methods of thought that move backwards, inferring from effects to their possible causes or reasons. This procedure of thought consists in beginning with how something appears within experience in order then to seek the reason, meaning or cause of this object: the reason for an action, the meaning of a dream, the cause of an event.

Deleuze calls this procedure of inference from experience 'representation'. It is called representation because it consists in beginning with a representation, a model of the object as this object appears. Deleuze develops an elaborate account of representation based, on the one hand, on Aristotelian logic and, on the other, on the theories of understanding presented by Descartes and Kant. Conventionally, in the history of philosophy one separates Aristotle from Descartes and Kant because the former views language and thought as implying a direct mirror relation between the subject predicate structure of thought (and language) and the structure of objects and their properties within physical reality; by contrast, Descartes and Kant hold that the objects of our thought and knowledge are at one remove from physical reality. We think about ideas (Descartes) or phenomena (Kant) but we are not able to say that or whether these ideas and phenomena necessarily map the actual structure of the world.

For Deleuze there is, however, a common principle that unites Aristotle, on the one hand, and Descartes and Kant, on the other, namely, the principle that thought begins with something – an object, an idea, a phenomenon – that is given or, better, *represented* in experience. Thinking is then viewed as a process of reasoning, starting from and grounded in this experience. The representational philosophy of thought and knowledge consists in laying bare the structure of this reasoning activity and its relation to experience.

It is this entire picture of thought, experience and the philosophy of knowledge (epistemology) that Deleuze now calls 'representation' and which he opposes to immanence.

The basic difference between the two ways of conceiving thought and its place in reality concerns the notions of the 'object' of philosophical thought itself. For Deleuze, the 'object' is something that has an inner genetic cause. For the philosophy of representation the object is something that is represented within experience. Thought is for Deleuze an activity that takes place within reality; it is a process that unfolds amidst other processes. The highest form of thought is the genetic articulation of immanent processes. For the philosophers of representation, thinking is an articulation of or making explicit what is already given as a representation in experience. The genetic and immanent understanding sought by Deleuze is not grounded in experience and its objects do not necessarily bear a strong resemblance to empirical objects.

The initial metaphysical intuition of Deleuze is very simple; the vital forces that can be activated in thought are kept at bay by an ordering and filtering system which imposes on reality a determinate logical structure. We may move beyond this logical structure if we can produce thoughts that are sufficiently abstract to think reality outside of representation. Deleuze's general account of what it is to be, or 'ontology', therefore leads to a perspective on human life that is in conflict with conscious experience. However, Deleuze also seeks to replace this conscious subject with another subject, defined by its passage through time, its capacity to undergo affects and by its creative potentials rather than its conscious experience of itself.

This book thus sees Deleuze as an anti-Platonist of a particular, paradoxical kind: someone who criticizes Plato while sharing very many of his assumptions about philosophy. Common to Plato and Deleuze is an ambition for philosophy to be able to go beyond common sense and everyday experience, to present a perceptive on the world that may challenge how it presents itself within experience. For Deleuze, this includes distancing himself from a many of the assumptions about thought and reality developed within the modern philosophical tradition. In particular, he is seeking to provide an alternative to the so-called concept of the *subject*, the notion of the individual human mind as constituting a self-conscious centre of knowledge and action.

However, Deleuze's philosophy also contains the germs of an alternative subject or concept of the subject. This alternative subject would not be founded in self-consciousness and rational mental capabilities but on the temporal and creative passage that a human being may undergo either in the field of its own life or in the more restricted fields of thought and writing. The mapping of this alternative subject is the most concrete application and realization of the principle of immanence: the alternative subject, being not defined by self-awareness, is immanent within its own acts. Deleuze calls this alternative subject, first, the embryonic subject (*sujet larvaire*), then the 'nomadic subject', and finally, in the Kafka book and in *A Thousand Plateaus*, 'becoming'. In Deleuze's thought, the starting-point for formulating this alternative concept of the subject is the concept of 'affect'. According to Deleuze, affects are the basic components of mental activity. Now the concept of an affect does not entail the concept of subjective self-awareness. To understand an affect is to see it as a *force*, a particular type of energy and this energy does not presuppose self-consciousness. The questions we may ask about affects are: how do they combine? What affects is the mind capable of? What thoughts are generated by affects? In this philosophical perspective, the mind is a site of thoughts rather than a centre of consciousness. These thoughts are not defined by the fact that someone can say: they are my thoughts. Thoughts, in other words, are not defined as *belonging to a subject*. Deleuze's books on Hume, Nietzsche and Spinoza each develop a particular aspect of this affect psychology and attack a specific dimension of the concept of the subject in its Cartesian or Kantian versions.

Historical Background

Deleuze's work was produced during a 40-year period, stretching from the mid-1950s to the early 1990s. When Deleuze began writing as a philosopher, French academic philosophy was dominated, on the one hand, by the discovery of the German philosophers Hegel, Husserl and Heidegger, and, on the other, by a specifically French school of *history* of philosophy. It was the latter trend that initially had the strongest impact on Deleuze's development as a philosopher.

According to this school, the history of philosophy seeks to display the intrinsic truth of each philosophical system of the past, that is, show each system in as favourable a light as possible, when required, by strengthening the internal coherence of that system. The task of the historian of philosophy is therefore not to explain how a philosopher came to develop particular concepts or problems, but to interpret the system of that philosophy in view of making it rationally valid, and if necessary to reconstruct the system so that it appears to conform, in the best possible way, to its own premises.[4] This historical school was represented, for instance, by Martial Guéroult, Victor Goldschmidt and Jules Vuillémin. They all ranged widely in their interests, writing on philosophers from different periods and movements, a trait that Deleuze adopted.

Deleuze began his career in this historical school but was not insensitive to the intellectual climate of his time, dominated by the interpretation of Hegel, Husserl and Heidegger. Some of his first texts are thus reviews of works of existential philosophy and psychology in the Heideggerian tradition.[5] Nevertheless, the early philosophy of Deleuze consists of a series of short monographs, three of which were devoted to Hume, Bergson and Nietzsche, philosophers who were not part of this intellectual climate and who were pursuing a different kind of project from that of Hegel, Husserl or Heidegger. Deleuze also wrote on the two philosophers Spinoza and Kant, who, while not being directly linked to either phenomenology or Hegelian philosophy, were by no means unknown to the French academic tradition, where since the nineteenth century they had been considered as epitomizing philosophical reason. During this period Deleuze also wrote book-length essays on the writers Marcel Proust and Sacher Masoch.

Through these texts, Deleuze presents himself as a sophisticated and original historian of philosophy, practising the French reconstructive method of interpretation – which he at the same time refines in a particular way: he condenses his own arguments and mode of exposition in the extreme, thereby eliding the question of where his own philosophy takes over and the interpretation becomes a reconstruction. Thus, in all these works, he primarily develops concepts that subsequently become part of his own philosophy. He gives expression to this philosophy in the two parallel works published in the late 1960s, *Difference and Repetition*, and *The Logic of Sense*.

In the 1950s, French philosophy was at a crossroads between two very different schools of thought, that of *phenomenology* and that of *structuralism*. Phenomenology was the older of the two movements. From the 1930s to the 1950s, French philosophy had been dominated by existential and phenomenological thinkers such as Jean-Paul Sartre, Maurice Merleau-Ponty and Gabriel Marcel. Drawing on a set of interlinked influences – Hegel, Kierkegaard, Husserl and Heidegger – this generation had agreed on a common set of philosophical concerns. Philosophy was to be answerable to the basic fact of human *existence*. It should not be a merely rational enterprise but should have something to say about how we exist, how we live and die, how we confront the world of things around us.

This existential phenomenology marked a break with the academic tradition of French philosophy which had been predominantly concerned with the history of science and the history of philosophy itself. The following generation, that of Michel Foucault, Jacques Derrida and Gilles Deleuze, marks a return to this earlier historical orientation, but, at the same time, these philosophers evolved through a critical debate with existential phenomenology, and therefore sought to maintain the aim of this tradition to be relevant to ethical, aesthetic and political questions.

Phenomenology itself, as a discipline within philosophy, began with the German philosopher Edmund Husserl at the end of the nineteenth century. Phenomenology gave itself the task of testing and assessing the claims made by various sciences, and in particular the claims made within the formal or pure sciences of logic and mathematics. Following Kant, Husserl believed that the validity of arguments within these sciences was in need of a special kind of justification which these sciences themselves would not be able to provide, and which could only be made by philosophy. Philosophy was therefore to be considered as the science of all the other sciences, a kind of superior science. The object of this superior science was truth and validity, or rather the *meaning* of truth and validity. A logical inference might be valid according to the rules of logic, but what does it *mean* that it is valid?

In order to answer this question, Husserl analysed the experience that we have of something being true. He thought that if we pay close attention to the mental acts involved in any experience of truth, we will understand the universal properties of any argument that produces knowledge. In the course of this examination of mental acts, he gradually came to widen his area of study until it concerned all the ways in which something may appear to consciousness, and all the different kinds of conscious experience there can be, from fleeting sensations to formal arguments. Phenomenology thereby came to develop a new method for *describing conscious experience.* It was this method which was adopted by Husserl's followers in France.

French phenomenology developed this method in a psychological direction and sought to determine the specific differences between different types of conscious acts and behaviour. This method entailed the assumption that any activity or social phenomenon should be understood as *something that appears within conscious experience.*

The generation of Foucault, Derrida and Deleuze attacked this French existential and psychological school of phenomenology under three headings. For them, existential phenomenology consisted of a *vocabulary*, a *method* and an *agenda*. Its vocabulary was centred on the terms 'consciousness', 'existence' and 'subjectivity'. Its method was to examine psychological phenomena, language and art from the point of view of conscious, subjective experience. Its agenda was what became known as *humanism.*[6]

They took issue with phenomenology on all of these levels. They thought it would be necessary to forge an entirely new vocabulary for philosophy, a vocabulary which would not refer to, or depend on, a notion of subjective experience. This vocabulary would be produced by new methods of philosophical enquiry, which would be completely separate from introspection and psychological description. Thereby philosophy would also become free of the 'anthropocentric' perspective and its humanist agenda. They sought to attack humanism, i.e. an anthropocentric and individualistic perspective on the mind, on language, and reality as a whole, through the analysis and construction of formal structures that would not depend on the notion of such a subjective and individualistic point of view.

A central term in the new vocabulary is derived from debates in literary criticism at the time. It is the concept of the *sign*. This concept came to stand for an entirely new approach to literature and language – far beyond the relatively modest weight of the term itself. The concept of the 'sign' is old and has been discussed by many philosophers, but never as a concept designating a central philosophical problem or concern.

The Swiss linguist Ferdinand de Saussure proposed a linguistic theory based on the concept of the sign at the beginning of the twentieth century. He used the concept of the sign as a strategic term that would allow him to formulate a scientific theory of language. He did so by isolating the 'system' of language (*langue*) from the use of language within communication (*parole*), as he thought it was necessary for the demarcation of linguistics as a discipline to identify a kind of meaning that would be completely internal to language.

This internal meaning, which he calls 'signification', is the relation between an acoustic image (*signifier*) and a conceptual meaning (*signified*). The composition of signifier, signified and signification is a *sign*. The sign in turn does not derive its power to signify from its relation to anything outside of language such as an object it could be used to refer to. The sign is invested with signification by standing in a differential relation to other signs within the language system.

The anthropologist Claude Lévi-Strauss and the psychoanalyst Jacques Lacan had started appropriating Saussure's ideas during the 1940s and 1950s. In the 1960s, their texts became influential in many other human and social sciences in France and became a shaping force in the cultural climate of the time.

The application of Saussure's method led in two different but related directions of research. On the one hand, it produced an attempt to describe, within different fields of cultural practice, self-enclosed formal systems that would then be seen as *unconscious rules* governing that practice. This general trend is what became known as 'structuralism'. On the other hand, Saussure's theory of the sign produced the research programme known as 'semiotics'.

The theory and research programme of semiotics aimed at studying systems of communication, and, in particular, literature, according to cultural invariants, such as recurrent narrative patterns. These cultural invariants were seen to organize the narrative or semantic possibilities of literary texts in the same way that the language system, according to Saussure, defines the possibility of language use for individual speakers.[7]

In the French cultural climate of the 1960s, the conjunction of structuralism and semiotics seemed immensely promising. It opened up the prospect of studying the whole range of cultural practices according to unconscious formal rules. This appeared to be at the same time both scientifically rigorous and in tune with contemporary experimental writing, which also relied on formal and abstract structures. If one could write novels that would not have conscious experience at their core, but develop much more abstract and formal patterns of description, such as was the case for instance in the novels of Marguerite Duras and Alain Robbe-Grillet, then this would have its parallel in the attempt by the human sciences to describe language, literature, cinema or the unconscious without reference to individual conscious experience. There is thus a point of convergence between science and experimental writing originating in the notion that a formalist method of analysis, whether practised in science or in literature, would make the humanist concept of the subject superfluous and obsolete.

At this point of convergence one could further envisage the much more drastic and general philosophical prospect of *overcoming* humanism, i.e. of destroying the very notion of the human being as a conscious centre of thought and action. This philosophical anti-humanism was embraced by the generation of philosophers who included Derrida, Foucault and Deleuze. It celebrated the destruction of the subject with a paradoxical pathos of liberation. To better understand this project of liberation, we have to look more closely at the notion of the subject itself and its possible 'critique'.

Post-structuralism and the Critique of the 'Subject'

The philosophies of Foucault, Derrida and Deleuze, as well as theories of literature produced in the 1970s by Roland Barthes and others, are sometimes referred to in the English-speaking world as 'post-structuralism'. This term is both helpful and misleading. The philosophers referred to are 'post'-structuralist rather than structuralist, because structuralism is a research programme aiming to introduce standards of formal rigour into the human sciences and this is not a primary concern of these thinkers. They are also 'post'-structuralist in a chronological sense. One can see in the works of Foucault and Deleuze, for instance, a change in method and orientation occurring around 1970: in the wake of the '68 movement one witnesses a move away from the preoccupation with formal systems of books like Deleuze's *Proust and Signs* (1964) and Foucault's *The Order of Things* (1966) towards political themes that become prominent in works such as Foucault's *Discipline and Punish* (1975) and Deleuze and Guattari's *Anti-Oedipus* (1972). A third meaning of 'post' in post-structuralism concerns the term 'structure' itself. This term had already been questioned by both Deleuze and Derrida in the 1960s, in quite similar ways, for implying a rationalistic and metaphysical notion of order which they sought to question – Derrida with the concept of 'writing', Deleuze with the concept of a 'series', both terms referring to processes or relations that cannot be encapsulated within the notion of a closed 'structure'.[8]

At the same time, however, the term 'post-structuralism' is problematic because it overstates the similarities between these thinkers and induces one to believe in a shared agenda, for instance, a project of undermining positivism within the university or a shared idea of what constitutes philosophy. However, these thinkers did not form a post-structuralist 'school' based on shared principles or a shared canon of texts that they would work from.

Thus, Foucault comes from the tradition of history of science and religion (Canguilhem, Dumézil),[9] Derrida works within the horizon of Heidegger's philosophy and Deleuze continues the cosmological and metaphysical tradition of the Stoics, Spinoza, Leibniz, Bergson and Nietzsche.

The notion of a 'critique of the subject', which can be applied to all three, is thus, first of all, defined by the concept of the subject that they all attack. This concept of the subject is initially epistemological. It is the principle, common to Descartes and Kant, that the truth of an idea or a judgement can be assessed through a process of critical examination of the idea or judgement by the conscious mind itself. Descartes and Kant thus locate epistemological questions within a space of *self-reflection*. This in turn defines the *philosophy of the subject* as a particular kind of method. This method begins in Descartes, is refined by Kant, and culminates in the phenomenology of Husserl. All these thinkers propose methods of *systematic* – and not merely psychological – self-reflection. The philosophy of the subject thus consists in a series of methods: Cartesian analysis of ideas, Kantian transcendental analysis of faculties, phenomenological analysis of acts of consciousness.

For Deleuze, this epistemological subject is historically dependent on a wider moral and cultural notion of subjectivity which evolved within Christianity and was analysed by Nietzsche. According to Nietzsche, in Deleuze's interpretation, Christianity produced a new kind of *inner life* based on the idea of moral self-evaluation, the ascription of values to one's own actions and the reflection upon those values within a space of moral conscience. In French, it is the same word 'conscience' which denotes what English refers to by the two words 'consciousness' and 'conscience'. In the Christian subject, consciousness and conscience form a strong alliance, setting up within each mind a moral judge scrutinizing its own thoughts and actions.[10] Next to the technical, epistemological definition of the subject, and the broad cultural and moral definition of subjectivity in Christianity, the term has a third context of significance, which is the rationalist philosophy of the Enlightenment.

In the philosophy of the Enlightenment, the ability of human beings to develop reason, self-reflection and self-conscious responsibility both as individuals and in their political communities was seen as a means of overcoming the burdens of ignorance and social injustice. The Enlightenment subjects are autonomous, morally and politically responsible individuals who shape their own lives, as opposed to being governed by custom and authority. The Enlightenment subject is thus understood as the condition for a certain kind of historical progress, namely the progress of reason and justice, generated by critical rational subjects scrutinizing inherited social and cultural norms. The 'attack on the subject', therefore immediately concerns the entire Cartesian, Kantian and phenomenological programme of self-reflection, the Christian morality of self-scrutiny and the Enlightenment programme of critical rationalism and the belief in political progress.

Of these three dimensions of the concept of the subject, it is the programme of enlightened rationalism that French philosophers of Deleuze's generation opposed most directly. This hostility originates in previous generations of philosophy, and especially it has roots in the thought of Friedrich Nietzsche, Georges Bataille and Maurice Blanchot, three thinkers who exercised a strong influence on French philosophers in the 1960s.

Nietzsche and Bataille share a perspective on human life that is completely different from that of the philosophy of the subject, with its belief in the central role of human consciousness and its ties to the programme of the Enlightenment. The perspective presented by Nietzsche and Bataille is neither based on an analysis of consciousness, nor wedded to the Enlightenment notion of scientific and cultural progress. It is a perspective that consists of examining culture, psychology, science and politics from outside the perspective that emerges from conscious experience, individual action and the temporal horizon of individual lives. Thus, for Nietzsche, the human being is a certain kind of animal conditioned by cultural and historical forces. For Bataille, the life of modern bourgeois society masks a level of deeper spiritual and sexual energy that, ultimately, constitutes the ground of society.

Nietzsche and Bataille share two premises in particular which make them different from philosophers of the Enlightenment. They see the contemporary age of science and democracy within a very long-term historical perspective that seems to relativize the merits

of science and democracy. Second, they do not see the achievements
of this contemporary rationalistic and democratic society as positive
achievements. Rather, they problematize the present, modern age,
suggesting that modern subjectivity and rationality have come to
dominate our inner worlds and our political culture by covering up
a more direct experience of existence, of vital energy, of sexuality
or of death, experiences that would have been enacted in Greek
tragedy or in certain forms of ritual. These experiences of excess or
of loss of self and individual identity are suppressed in modern
society since they would undermine the rational self-conscious
subject if it were to be subjected to them.[11] Thus, both Nietzsche and
Bataille suggest that something has got lost in the processes of
Enlightenment and modernization. What Nietzsche calls 'tragedy'
and Bataille refers to as the 'inner life' are modes of experiencing
the world which are not hedged in by rationality in any form,
whether moral, political or scientific. This notion that there is a
dimension of existence that is essential to us, but which we have
nevertheless covered up or lost touch with, and which we therefore
need to reclaim, is adopted by both Foucault and Deleuze. This
existential dimension, however, is not to be thought of in the terms
of 'existential' philosophy within the categories of *subjectivity* such
as anxiety, freedom of choice. Rather, it should be possible to recover
this existential dimension without referring to a self-conscious
subject.

There are for Deleuze and Foucault two areas where this other
existential dimension is expressed: sexuality and modern literature
– and often one in conjunction with the other. Foucault devoted
an important section of *The Order of Things* to the works of the
Marquis de Sade, whereas Deleuze wrote two long essays on erotic
literature, one on Sacher Masoch and one on Pierre Klossowski. In
their conception of literature and sexuality as opening up a special
kind of experience, Foucault and Deleuze are again influenced by
Bataille who created the notion that sexuality is a stage on which
the subject is potentially *displaced* from itself, loses its bearings, and
thereby gains access to a different openness to the world. However,
the movement beyond modern rationality in literature is not confined to the expression or enactment of sexuality. Thus, another
French thinker, Maurice Blanchot, believed this loss of subjectivity
to be the substance of literature itself. He thought that literature
defines a space outside of morality, reason and subjective self-
mastery.[12] The literary text enacts a movement away from rational

and lucid existence towards what he calls the *neutral* ('le neutre'). The neutral is a mode of being that is not organized by rational divisions and distinctions. This concept of the neutral became very important to Deleuze as he developed his own version of this concept in *The Logic of Sense*.

Foucault and Deleuze each formulate their own ideas of freedom by continuing the tradition of Bataille with his notion of inner life as a loss of self, and of Blanchot, with his concept of the neutral as a sphere of indistinction or indifferentiation. Foucault calls this freedom *the space of the outside* – outside meaning the outside of what we can rationally master. Deleuze and Guattari have many names for this freedom but the two most important are 'schizophrenia' and the 'line of flight'. In *Anti-Oedipus*, schizophrenia is presented as one such mode of being 'outside' the rational system of differentiation. In *A Thousand Plateaus*, they define freedom as a 'line of flight' that would begin within well-defined social groups and behaviour but then take off in an unknown direction, moving towards as yet unmapped territories, outside of conscious planning and previously known values.

The main critical thrust of Deleuze and Guattari's philosophy can thus be framed within the search for an *Other* perspective, beyond the anthropocentric horizon of thought that we derive from ordinary experience. They seek to provide a perspective on human life and political reality which does not put the human being or its conscious mental activity at the centre of that reality. This constitutes an 'Other' perspective that requires a speculative leap, a move within thought beyond experience, and hence a very abstract viewpoint on human life. One critical question for Deleuze in this context is how the search for another subject than the subject of consciousness, and the description of creative development that is not dependent on consciousness relates to the problem of freedom.

The English word 'freedom' and the French word 'liberté' do not imply any notion of unconscious layers of experience. Political freedom is evident and visible in its absence as much as when it is fought for. The legal and moral concept of freedom contained in the notions of individual responsibility refers to relations between agents and their acts within an observable social world. Someone is responsible for an action if the action can be uniquely correlated with that person as its cause. Underlying these political and legal notions of freedom there is, however, the more intractable metaphysical question concerning conscious autonomy or the 'freedom

of the will': is it possible for an action ever to be the direct consequence of a conscious decision?

Deleuze's philosophy does not address any of these political,
moral or metaphysical issues concerning freedom, but the concept
of becoming as a creative line of flight entails a problem, if not a
well-defined concept, of freedom. We will touch upon this problem
of freedom at different points in the following discussion.

1

Immanence and Subjectivity

Immanence and Representation

The two central concepts in Deleuze's philosophy, according to the interpretation that I propose in this book, are 'immanence' and 'representation'. These terms are, we might say, strategic terms and building blocks in Deleuze's thinking.

Immanence designates what is desirable for philosophy, a task and a goal. Immanence is thus, first of all, a way of thinking. What it is to think immanently is, however, easier to define negatively than positively. It is *not* to think from the point of view of a transcendent God – in the history of philosophy, the term 'immanence' is used to describe metaphysical systems such as that of Spinoza, in which God is identical with and thus internal to or 'immanent within' reality. However, in relation to this classical notion of immanence as opposed to transcendence, Deleuze formalizes the term so that it comes to mean *any manner of thinking that dispenses with an external or transcendent viewpoint*. In different contexts, this has different implications.

For the *ontology of the mind*, immanence means that the mind is part of reality and unfolds as an activity within the force field of reality as a whole. There can be no subject situated outside of the natural system of causes (in the manner, for instance, of Kant's 'transcendental subject' of experience). In its appropriation of Nietzsche and Bergson, the philosophy of Deleuze will seek to define a subject of concrete temporal processes, or becoming (Bergson) and a subject of active affect and self-affirmation (Nietzsche).

For *epistemology*, or the examination of what it is to think well and of how thought relates to its objects, the concept of immanence entails the view that thought develops as a process alongside the reality that it seeks to grasp: thought is not like a picture of a world of objects, but the unfolding of different kinds of reality within the reality of thought.

The problem of how we should live the concept of immanence leads to an opposition between ethics and morality: Deleuze's ethics, inherited from Spinoza, is concerned with the affirmation and liberation of one's active i.e. joyous affects and with the acquisition of a perspective of one's life from the point of view of destiny that consists in seeing one's life as an immanent and inevitable variation of forces. Morality, on the other hand, consists of a system of *judgement* geared towards an evaluation of actions. According to Deleuzian ethics, such a system of moral judgement represents action in isolation from the system of forces that they express.

In this book we will follow the interconnections between these three strands: the ontology or description of reality as a self-generating system; epistemology – that is, the discussion of how thought arises within reality and how, in turn, it can and should articulate reality through concepts; and, finally, ethics – the contemplation of our own place in reality as individual beings existing in time.

From this principle of immanence Deleuze further derives a critique of *humanism* or the anthropocentric perspective. Thought and language are approached from a cosmological perspective in which human life appears as a relatively limited process unfolding among much larger processes that it will never fully be able to master intellectually. This cosmological and anti-humanist perspective is then opposed to an anthropocentric conception of thought, which he calls 'representation'. Within representation, intellectual activity is at the service of common sense and ordinary conscious experience. The main proponents of this common-sense conception of thought, according to Deleuze, are Aristotle, Descartes and Kant. They have different notions of what experience and thinking consist of, but they all seek to limit the speculative ambitions of thought by referring to shared conscious experience and common sense.

The term 'representation' used in this critical way has its origin in German philosophy, in the Idealist philosophy of Hegel and in Heidegger's philosophy of being. In his critique of Kant, Hegel accused him of conceiving of logical categories in a formal and abstract way, thus separating them from their actuality in the life of thought. He also accuses him of relying on a limited concept of logic (the logic of understanding or *Verstand*) confined within the subject-predicate model inherited from Aristotle and which cannot grasp the life of thought as reason (*Vernunft*).[1]

According to Heidegger, the tradition of philosophy has repeatedly masked the truth of being by identifying being with a particular kind of being, namely the being of the physical 'object' that is present before the mind. This has produced an objectifying and theoretical concept of reality, manifest both in the subject-predicate logic of Aristotle and in Descartes' mathematical theory of physical nature.

Hegel and Heidegger thus both oppose a philosophical grasp of reality – the life of thought as reason, being as it would disclose itself outside of a scientific objectification – to a limited and limiting form of thought that, as it were, interposes itself between us and the world in the manner of a filter. This is equally Deleuze's notion of representation.

Let us now look at the most important passage where Deleuze defines representation. There he connects two themes: the notion of an indirect or 'mediated' grasp of reality and the notion of a classification and identification of objects by the use of the instruments of logic as these were defined by Aristotle. Deleuze defines representation with regard to the most basic relationship between existing things, the relation of difference in order to make the distinction between a direct grasp of difference, i.e. a grasp of difference as such, and a mediated representation of difference in terms of a logical grid of classification.

What is at stake in this question of philosophical method is the ontological problem of what constitutes the most fundamental character of being. If 'to be' is to be a 'thing', belonging to a certain kind or species of things, then for something to acquire reality is to be determined as belonging within such a classification. In other words, if reality is divided up into definable things which stand in an ordered relations to one another, then there is a strict mirror relationship between, on the one hand, the order that we may impose on the world through classification and comparison between things and, on the other, the actual order that exists in the world. This mirror relation is characterized in the vocabulary of ontology by the term 'determination': the thing is *determined* as being what it is through the same relations that we identify when we determine what the thing is, in thought. Due to this mirror relationship, the concept of determination is the key to understanding the philosophical tradition of representation. Representation, in its original

Aristotelian form, presupposes a mirror relationship between thought, language and world, centred on the concept of the individual physical thing. Determination corresponds to this model. It characterizes a process of applying concepts to objects as these objects are represented in thought.

In themselves, these concepts are merely abstract and general, that is, they are *indeterminate*, as they do not yet refer to a particular object. The thing that is to be determined is only determined when it is identified as belonging to a particular species. This species in turn is situated within a classificatory system, a hierarchy of kinds or *genera*, going from the most general to the most specific. A dog, for instance, is a dog of a certain race, then it is a member of the species 'dogs'; the species of dogs is itself part of the genus of mammals, which is part of the genus of animals, which is part of the genus of living beings until one reaches the point of the most general genera or *determinables*. The definition of the individual thing, once it has been assigned to a species, requires us to list its essential and defining properties. These properties are the *determinations* of the thing. The thing that is defined through this movement of identification, classification and definition has now been completely determined.

The movement from the indeterminate concept via the determinable general kinds through the determining properties to the determined object is a movement which serves to identify, to fixate and to situate all at once, so that the specificity of the thing, its difference from others, is entirely rational and intelligible in terms of a larger scheme of classification of the world and in terms of the relations between the various parts of that system. This classificatory and determinative system of thought at the same time opens a set of relations within thought between different parts of the classificatory system. These formal relations form the basic objects of rational thought.

These basic rational relations are '*identity*' (given by the concept that defines a kind of thing), '*analogy*' (relations between the most general abstract terms), '*opposition*' (the mutually excluding properties that define the border between two species of the same genus), and '*resemblance*' (the observable likeness of individual objects belonging to the same kind).

Let us now look at the dense passage from *Difference and Repetition* where Deleuze summarizes the process of determination and the system of representation of difference that it corresponds to:

There are four principal aspects to 'reason' in so far as it is the medium of representation: identity, in the form of the *undetermined* concept; analogy, in the relation between ultimate *determinable* concepts; opposition, in the relation between *determinations* within the concept; resemblance, in the *determined* object of the concept itself. These forms are like the four heads or the four shackles of mediation. 'Difference' is 'mediated' to the extent that it is subjected to the four-fold root of identity, opposition, analogy and resemblance.[2]

In order to escape this Aristotelian model of mediation and deter-mination through classification, philosophical thought has to move along a completely different route where the mental act of identify-ing objects and making judgements about them are not seen to be the prototypical operations of the mind. Deleuze's philosophy is both the theorization and the demonstration of this alternative tra-jectory of philosophy.

This alternative route involves questioning the notion of 'inten-tionality' or directedness that is implicit in the notion of 'judge-ment', the notion that thought always requires and is correlated with determinate objects. For Deleuze, philosophical thought should be understood from the inside of this thought itself as a relation to objects that are themselves constructed or 'developed' within thought. Deleuze calls these thought-internal objects 'problems'. The problem is an object that can only be thought and can never be given in perception. This mode of thinking thus acquires a high level of *abstraction*. This is one of the most central claims made by Deleuze.

For Deleuze, the way out of the limitations imposed by subject-predicate logic thus does not reside in some kind of intuition or feeling but, on the contrary, in an exacerbated form of abstraction, a state where thought has become more formal, more abstract than the subject-predicate model itself. For only then is it possible to articulate relations of difference directly without having to rely on representational structures of classification. This strong emphasis on abstraction moves Deleuze close to the metaphysical Idealism of Plato.

Platonism and Anti-Platonism

Deleuze's aspiration to conquer a completely abstract perspective on reality moves his philosophy within the orbit of Plato's meta-physical Idealism. For Plato also sought to establish a perspective on thought and reality that would not be derived from experience. At the same time, Deleuze will define himself in direct opposition to Plato. For it is as if Plato for Deleuze is the chosen enemy, the perfect negative mirror, and that measuring himself with Platonism allows him also to find a route out of subjectivity and conscious experience.

For the concept of *immanence* is formulated not only in opposition to the representational mode of grasping reality but also in relation to what we may call 'Platonism'. Deleuze often refers to Platonic doctrines as a counter-point to his own philosophy, but he also recognizes that the relationship to what he thereby rejects is ambivalent: 'The task of modern philosophy has been defined: to overturn Platonism. That this overturning should conserve many Platonic characteristics is not only inevitable but desirable.'[3] The Platonic traits that Deleuze may himself repeat stem from his attempt to reach a level of abstraction from which to describe reality independently of representation. For representation is not just a logical process of classification, it is also couched within sense experience.

Representation contains the belief that sense experience exhibits its own logical structure.[4] It is this perceived necessary connection between logical thought and sense experience – sometimes referred to by Deleuze as the harmony of the mental faculties in Kant – that makes representation into a self-limitation of thought. The aim of philosophy is, therefore, as we saw earlier, to achieve an 'Other', more abstract perspective on reality than the one we naturally and spontaneously have when we extrapolate from our own experience.

The belief in abstraction also corresponds to the structuralist and semiotic movement of the time, but Deleuze's approach to abstraction is entirely different from that of Lévi-Strauss or Foucault, for instance. Deleuze is concerned to identify the formal principles that account for the genesis of reality but these principles are taken to be *internal* to reality. This is a much more metaphysical programme than that of any of Deleuze's contemporary structuralist or post-structuralist philosophers – and it is this metaphysics that brings Deleuze's philosophy close to the Platonic tradition.

For Platonism does not imply or promote the self-limitation of thought produced in 'representation'. It is a speculative philosophy that does not take sense experience to be a measure of truth – and Deleuze too is a speculative philosopher. Thus, Deleuze, like Plato, attempts to provide, with the instruments of thinking alone, an account of reality that differs markedly from what we would think reality is if we trust sense experience and ordinary language use. But the nature of this speculative account at the same time differs sharply from Plato's rationalistic Idealism.

To Plato, reality, or what counts as real, is always what can be *known*. Knowledge is the possession in the mind of an ideal structure that perfectly matches reality. If thought can produce an adequate description of reality, it is therefore only because reality already has been defined as having a stable, knowable form that lends itself to such a philosophical description. This opens up a question of what reality must be in order to fit this ideal description. This problem was addressed by Plato in his dialogue *Parmenides*. There he raises the question of whether a philosophical description of reality, a description which would be based on the knowledge of a set of ideal and eternal forms, would comprise everything that we encounter in experience or only part of what we experience as making up the material world:

> And what about these, Socrates – they would really seem ridiculous: hair and mud and dirt, for example, or anything else which is utterly worthless and trivial. Are you perplexed whether or not one should say that there is a separate form for each of these too, a form that again is other than the sorts of things our hands touch?[5]

Countering this obstacle, Plato argues that reality in itself is an abstract intelligible structure distinct from the material world we encounter in experience. He infers from this notion of an intelligible structure that reality in itself must be *static*, since what is changing does not conform to any single description. Ideal realities can, by contrast, be known perfectly since they are not changeable. The starting point for Deleuze's theory of being and thought is the affirmation of the opposite pole of Plato's dilemma: not 'what must reality be to be knowable?' but 'what must thought be, if reality is in constant flux and consists primarily of processes?'

If we consider Deleuze's philosophy as a whole, we may say that Deleuze uses three basic terms to describe reality, ontological concepts which determine what it means to be. These terms are *difference*, *multiplicity* and *becoming*. Each of these terms is defined in opposition to Plato as they designate different kinds of opposites to the perfect and ideal identity of the Platonic forms. *Difference* is the primary trait of anything that is, in so far as any real existing being must be something new – and therefore different in relation to anything that existed before it came into being. Difference is therefore prior to identity, which is merely a function of how we name reality and represent it, by defining marks of identification and differentiation. Difference is not dependent on these marks of distinction as it is a feature of reality and not of our grasp of reality in thought.

The concept of *multiplicity* is for Deleuze primary in relation to *unity* because Deleuze argues that unity can only come into being from what was at first dispersed as a multiplicity. Finally, the notion of *becoming* is primary in relation to that of *stasis* since becoming is the actual character of reality as an interaction between the processes that reality consists of, whereas stasis is the character only of objects within some form of representation or ideal model.

This philosophical route via a critique of Plato opens for Deleuze a programme of speculative anti-Platonism, a metaphysics of the world as it is, in its diversity and transience. This, then, is also immanence: the requirement to account philosophically for the world as it is and not as it ought to be according to a Rational Ideal. At the same time of course, this account has to be philosophical; it cannot, if it is to be a critique of representation as well as of Platonism, use the categories we anyway use in experience.

Life of the Mind: Subject, Object, Affect

During the 1950s and early 1960s, Deleuze wrote four interrelated monographs in the history of philosophy devoted to Hume, Bergson, Nietzsche and Kant. Through these studies Deleuze develops a conception of the life of the mind as affect and activity. The mind is a bundle of affects because it is constantly affected by its environment. It is an activity, on the other hand, which is not limited in scope to this arena of interaction: we can think more than what we experience. These studies thus also trace a philosophical route between an empiricist conception of the mind as being essentially passive and a spiritualist conception of the mind as producing its own original kind of activity. The development of this philosophy of mind is embedded in a sustained critique of Kant's philosophy of knowledge or 'critique of reason'.

Kant's critical philosophy of reason is an analysis of what we may justifiably or legitimately know, what, in other words, we as rational; beings may claim to know about reality. As we as human beings exist in time and space and perceive the world through our senses,

we are constrained to know the world in a sensory way, as a phenomenal world, a world that appears to us in sense experience – this,
according to Kant, had not been sufficiently noted by rationalist
philosophers like Leibniz. Yet we are not simply passive in receiv-
ing sensory impressions from things around us – this notion of
passive impressions had been the basis for the empiricist theories
of knowledge proposed by Locke and Hume. We are not passive
since we order and rationally organize these impressions by applying categories and concepts to them. It follows from this, according
to Kant, that experience is *inherently rational*.

Kant believes experience to be fundamentally different from a
mere exposure to phenomenal reality: in order for things to at all
appear as things, i.e. as identifiable, separable, countable, distin-
guishable objects, they have first to be identified, separated, counted
and distinguished by us. Experience does not present us with things
which we then, subsequently, reason about. The things that we
perceive are only perceivable by us as the things they appear to be
because we organize sensory impressions in a certain way, by
applying categories of number, unity etc. to them as ordering rules.
Thus, experience does not just consist of impressions. Experience is
the field of intellectual and sensory activity where separate sense
impressions acquire the structure that we think of as a world made
up of objects. It is in this sense that experience is inherently rational.
According to Kant, we cannot conceive of an experience that is not
rationally ordered in this way.

The ultimate expression of this rationality within experience is
self-consciousness, which for Kant is the guarantee of the unity of
experience, the most basic justification for saying that our ordering
concepts are applicable to sense impressions. Deleuze's books on
Hume, Bergson and Nietzsche each attack a particular dimension
of this Kantian philosophy of rational, self-conscious experience.

Deleuze's early book on Hume announces the two concerns that
will guide his thought during the 1950s and 1960s. The first of these
problems regards the concept of the subject, the second regards the
role of affects in the life of the mind. These two problems are related
in a conception of the human mind as essentially passive, as a place
where affects take place rather than a centre of self-consciousness
and rationality.

The mind receives impressions and forms out of these impressions – or simple ideas – composite ideas. For this to be possible, the
mind needs to apply to its simple ideas a structuring force. This
structuring force consists for Hume in rules of association. For

Hume, these rules of association do not in themselves imply a rational activity. He studies the workings of the mind but he does not thereby seek to justify the beliefs that the mind produces. Unlike Kant, Hume does not claim that the task of philosophy is to show that experience embodies rational principles, but, on the contrary, to unmask what we hold to be rational principles as being mere conventions or mental habits. The mind comes to have certain beliefs because it is affected in a regular, habitual way, but it cannot invoke any universal rational principles to justify these beliefs, for the principles it would be able to invoke would themselves be derived from these mental habits.

Deleuze thus contrasts the Kantian concept of categories as rational rules leading to a justification of knowledge claims to Hume's quasi-mechanical principles of association generating composite ideas out of simple impressions but without leading to any justification of these ideas.

For Deleuze, Hume thereby proposes a concept of the subject that is entirely different from the Kantian rational and self-conscious unity of experience. The Humean subject is defined by a capacity to believe more than it is justified to believe on the basis of past sense experience. When we believe that the sun will rise again tomorrow, we don't actually know that it will, but we infer by induction from past experience that it will. In affirming that the sun will rise tomorrow, the mind goes beyond what it knows from the impressions it has received; it affirms something for which there is no direct perceptual evidence, no root in sense impressions.

For Kant, the subject is a rational and self-conscious unity of experience, serving as the ultimate justification of experience and empirical knowledge. The Humean subject, by contrast, does not serve to justify knowledge, since it is itself the result of an act of belief transcending knowledge. Through Hume, Deleuze is thus able to oppose the Kantian rational subject to a subject that emerges spontaneously from its own unjustifiable activity. This notion of a subject that is internal to its own activity rather than a principle of justification will be a thread running through all of Deleuze's philosophy. In particular, it is given expression in *Anti-Oedipus* with the concept of a nomadic subject that is also conceived as being inseparable from its own activity within the psyche.

With his work on the nineteenth-century philosopher Henri Bergson, Deleuze is able to develop a different, spiritualist account of mental activity and through this spiritualist philosophy to present another angle of attack on Kant. The spiritualist premise of

Bergson's philosophy involves the principle that mental activity is real, has a definite place within reality, and that it possesses an intrinsic unity that springs from its own unfolding as activity. In his first treatise, *Time and Free Will* (*Essai sur les données immédiates de la conscience*), Bergson explores how this spiritual reality of the mind appears to us within conscious experience. His second book, *Matter and Memory*, examines the relationship within conscious experience between perception and memory.

Deleuze finds in Bergson's philosophy a method of analysing the mind that is opposed to and challenges Kant's transcendental philosophy of cognitive faculties. For Kant, the cooperation of the faculties of reason, understanding, sensibility and imagination are necessary requirements for empirical knowledge. The transcendental method which seeks to determine the necessary requirements of knowledge does not study these faculties as actual or real psychological-spiritual activities, but as logical or formal presuppositions. Bergson, by contrast, examines the life of the mind as a reality, as a composite of distinct but intermingled activities. Thus, Bergson claims that within our normal experience the acts of perception and memory are always mixed but that in themselves, according to their own intrinsic natures as mental activities, they are clearly distinct and do not overlap. This means that conscious experience is a wholly inadequate source for understanding the components of experience. In other words, experience is not self-elucidating, we do not arrive at an understanding of experience by examining experience, but only by acquiring a rigorous method for separating mental acts from each other according to their own intrinsic natures. This method depends on a distinction between what is given in experience which Deleuze calls actuality, and the real natures of mental acts which are not given as such in actuality. These real natures only exist *virtually*.

The virtual existence of these natures is nevertheless real rather than a mere formal or logical presupposition of experience, but their reality is of a somewhat special kind. They inhabit a realm of existence which lies outside of the reality that we normally experience but this other reality at the same time conditions all the experience that we have since actual experience is a *composite* of the virtual natural natures of perception and memory.

According to Kant, we perceive physical nature within the bounds of space and time, and ourselves, our own inner states, in time only. Our inner states are thus phenomena just as much as physical nature appears as a series of phenomena. Neither the phenomena of 'outer sense' nor the phenomena of 'inner sense' can ever be perceived by us 'in themselves', i.e. independently of their conditions of appearance, as stretched out in time or as stretched out in time and space. We assume that our impressions are, in some sense, caused by external objects, but this causality falls outside of what we can rationally perceive and experience. In experience we can apply the concept of cause, at least the concept of a direct physical cause used in the science of physics, only to a succession of phenomena appearing in space. We are thus unable, within the bounds of experience, to understand our mental activity as real (the mind as spiritual substance or soul) and as causally related to the world around us or to the world as a whole.

This question of how to establish a causal connection between the life of the mind and the world around us is taken up by Nietzsche and reformulated. For Nietzsche, the mind is like a theatre of forces, a stage on which vital energies appear in various disguises, playing a variety of moral, psychological and cultural roles. The mind thus forms part of cultural history, not just of individual psychology. The ideas, emotions and turns of argument that occupy the individual mind do not belong to that individual mind alone, but are just played out there, staged by each individual in his or her own way, but having their origin elsewhere, within the cultural history of which the individual is part.

According to Deleuze, Nietzsche's method of cultural historical analysis of psychological and moral phenomena is grounded in a particular ontology of force. This notion of force is ambiguous, since it is not just a physical or mechanical quantity, but a quasi-spiritual energy *expressed as signification*. If the mind is a theatre, it is because forces that run through the individual and forces influencing the individual from the outside find expression in the mind as *signs*. Nietzsche thus develops a theory of signs or semiology and this semiology is based in a general cosmological theory of force. The mind is part of the world because the mind, like the world, is a system of forces.

This theory of force is further grounded in an ontological theory that Nietzsche defines by the terms 'will to power' and 'the eternal recurrence of the same'. Will to power is a reflexive and dynamic structure of force, a force that seeks its own growth. The eternal recurrence designates a cyclical point of view on the world located outside of the temporal span of individual lives and of family history, even outside of national cultural history.

Deleuze's interpretation of Nietzsche is based on a reconstruction of the ontology that is implied by these two terms. This reading allows Deleuze to introduce a problem that is opposed to Kantian philosophy at a much deeper level than that of Humean empiricism and Bergsonian spiritualism. This deeper level is that of a new genetic ontology and epistemology that Deleuze attributes to Nietzsche.

This genetic philosophy opposes the representational system of judgement both in its Aristotelian form and in its more sophisticated Kantian version, that is, the belief that our minds relate to the world by identifying objects and determining through judgement and by the use of logical criteria how each thing is different from and related to other things.

This genetic system of thought deduces the possibility of differences between forces from an ontological process that is prior to our knowledge and description of the world that we experience. This ontological process engenders difference out of itself without implying any structure that we could represent. Thus, the ontological process produces difference in a way that is alien to the way we identify difference within the system of judgement.

This ontology is articulated through the concepts of will to power and the eternal recurrence. Will to power is a first principle of difference. It is expressed as a principle for relating forces to one another, that is, through a process of selection, with a view to growth. In selecting one force over another, will to power does not obey criteria of choice or distinction. The selection is a self-defining process. Will to power is not a subject of this process. Will to power expresses itself as selection, and does not stand outside of selection as a judge or a subject. Eternal recurrence is a cosmological cycle of variation in which a stock of invariants are recycled, selected and combined in different combinations through history, thus engendering superficially different historical epochs and individual lives.

If, instead of judgement, the genetic principle of difference is the starting point for epistemology, then there is no assumption, as there is in the representational system of judgement, of a homogenous field of differences in which each difference can be exactly determined according to logical criteria.

Nietzsche has his own, genealogical, account of how we move from an affirmation of ourselves as will to power to a self-limitation of our thought within a homogenous field of representation. This genealogy opposes the pre-Socratic philosopher Heraclitus to the figure of Socrates. Heraclitus conceives of the mind as a *participation* in reality: what takes place in the mind is not of a fundamentally different nature from that which takes place in physical nature, as both the mind and the world are part of the same process of ongoing cosmic change. My life may seem very short in comparison to the mountain that I see at a distance, but it is the same fire that burns in both, in me and in the mountain, and which constitutes their being.

Heraclitus says:

> This (world-)order (*the same for all*) did none of gods or men make, but it always was and is and shall be: an everlasting fire, kindling in measures and going out in measures.
> For souls it is death to become water.[6]

Socrates, on the other hand, opposes thought to the world. Seeking to determine within thought essential moral properties such as courage in itself, wisdom in itself, etc., Socrates creates a space for the mind outside of any such all-encompassing process that would include both the world and our thoughts within it. This space consists of a position of judgement and evaluation, of comparing individual 'cases' or 'examples' to each other according to a common definition.

This Socratic conception of thought as judgement brings us back to Kant. For Kant is seen by Deleuze as the culmination of the philosophy of judgement within a philosophy of self-conscious subjectivity. In his study on Kant, Deleuze pays particular attention to the internal structure of judgement in Kant's philosophy. It is the outcome of our synthesis of sense impressions through the application of categories that we are able to identify and to recognize individual objects. Deleuze expresses this feature of judgement in the following way: 'That which constitutes knowledge is not simply the act by which the manifold is synthesized, but the act by which the represented manifold is related to an object (recognition: this is a table, this is an apple, this is such and such an object).'[7] Deleuze thus identifies a problem of reference in Kant: how is it that the series of impressions that I have can be made to refer to an identifiable individual object? He then argues that, for Kant, it is not just the synthesis of impressions with the aid of categories that establishes this reference to a specific individual, but that it depends on the mirror relation that Kant establishes between the unity of consciousness (apperception) and the unity of the object, considered as a general form of judgement, i.e. the object-form as a correlate of judgement. This mirror relation is the most complete version of representational thought. It contains a number of different principles:

1   Thought relates primarily to that which it can recognize as having the form of an individual object.
2   The object-form precedes any distinction between kinds of objects and is thus a mark of the homogeneity of the field of experience.
3   The unity of the object is inseparable from the unity of the self-conscious awareness of the unity of consciousness.

This representational model creates a strong correlation between the subject (self-conscious unity of experience) and object (the form of the object of judgement in general). It is this correlation between subject and object that most particularly characterizes the problem of the subject for Deleuze. His attempt at elaborating an alternative subject thus involves the task of separating the subjective and the objective poles of experience in order to relate them again at an ontological level that lies outside of conscious experience.

Now, regarding the Heraclitean model of thought presented in the Nietzsche book, of thought as participation in cosmic energy, this model offers a first, rudimentary version of such a split: the activity of thought is not evaluated by its content or what it is about, but by the forces that are active in it. Its relation to the world is therefore not a relation of intentionality, but a relation of participation in which the same forces that structure the world are active on the stage of consciousness. It will be an aim realized only in *A Thousand Plateaus* to account for the relationship between thought and reality in this way, such that thought is not defined by its objects, but by its interaction with forces around it.

Spinoza and the Principle of Immanence

Spinoza is perhaps the most important of Deleuze's interlocutors. It is through his study on Spinoza that Deleuze develops the principle of immanence that will define the parameters of the social theory he develops with Félix Guattari in *Anti-Oedipus*. In Spinoza, Deleuze also finds a critique of the philosophy of the subject as presented by Spinoza's contemporary, Descartes.

In his long treatise on Spinoza called *Spinoza and the Problem of Expression*, Deleuze primarily seeks to interpret the basic metaphysical structure of Spinoza's philosophy before showing the implications of this structure for an account of philosophical thought itself. Parallel to this conception of thought, Deleuze analyses

Spinoza's critique of the Cartesian philosophy of the subject, that is the philosophical method that consists in taking self-consciousness as a starting point for philosophy.

The problems that Deleuze addresses in his analysis of Spinoza's system thus concern, on one hand, the nature of philosophical thought and, on the other, the structure of being. To be is for Spinoza to belong to nature. The nature to which anything that is has to belong is a divine infinite substance. To belong to this substance means to be produced or generated by and within it. Substance itself is divine because it is a cause of itself; it is, in other words, self-generating. It is important for Deleuze that it is the same structure of being that governs both substance (which is infinite) and anything that is produced by substance (which is finite). Thus, the distinction between what is finite and what is infinite does not introduce a break or a discontinuity within being.

This sameness in the meaning of the term 'being' which is called its 'univocity' is a defining feature of Spinoza's principle of immanence. Univocity means that nothing, not even God, exists in a reality that would lie beyond the reality of the world, as a separate transcendent realm that we could only think about and refer to in indirect or symbolic terms. This attempt to avoid any transcendent or symbolic language becomes important later on, in Deleuze and Guattari's discussion of the writer Franz Kafka, who has often been read as employing a symbolic mode of writing or as writing towards an absent God. They argue in their essay *Kafka: Toward a Minor Literature* that everything in Kafka's texts is immanent, that nothing takes place on a different, transcendent plane of reality. The materialist theory of desire that is presented in *Anti-Oedipus* is likewise presented as an immanent, univocal structure, harbouring no secrets beyond its mode of functioning.

Spinoza's divine substance is also characterized by its way of functioning. Divine substance is characterized by producing an infinity of finite 'modes'. The human body and the human mind and all their activities are parts of this substance as modes – and they are parts in the particular sense of being produced by substance. The modes that a human being consists of exist within the 'attributes' of thought and extension. These attributes which divide and define human reality are at the same time the attributes of substance. Substance can only produce within definite attributes.

Through this process of production, the substance, according to Deleuze, expresses its own productive power in the modes that it produces. Within human beings this power is expressed through a certain fundamental desire (*conatus*), defined as a continuous effort to maintain and to strengthen, i.e. affirm, one's own existence. Following this principle of production and expression, if we now return to the epistemological question of how we examine our ideas, Spinoza, on this reading, states that we should in fact not examine our ideas, in the sense of reflecting upon them, but rather understand them as modes produced within reality, thus understand them from the outside, according to the genetic cause that is immanent within them, as a certain force of *conatus*.

In the correct order of reasoning, we must proceed from the cause to its effects, we must follow the genetic or expressive cause. In accordance with this conception of thought, an epistemological principle is formulated in the Spinoza book which will have consequences for all of Deleuze's subsequent work: We understand an object when we understand how it is being produced to the point of being able to reproduce the object in the mind. 'For explication, far from referring to the procedure of an intellect that remains external to the object, refers first of all to the development of the thing in itself, and in life.'[8] The genetic method consists in reproducing in the mind the process through which something was engendered within the productive process of reality as a whole. This genetic method constitutes a move beyond representation and the mapping of reality according to logical relations and a system of classification. It marks a direct relation to the principles by which reality is produced and through which it produces itself.

Deleuze presents Spinoza's philosophy through a confrontation between his genetic theory of internal causes and the concept of the subject in the philosophy of Descartes. Deleuze opposes Descartes and Spinoza at the level of method. He opposes the speculative and genetic method of Spinoza, which begins with an account of reality as a whole and then moves from that account to an analysis of the human mind and body, to the philosophy of Descartes, which starts with an analysis of the ideas that the mind is conscious of. Descartes starts his philosophical analysis from the notion of an individual human being who needs to learn how to reason well.[9]

Descartes holds that most of our ideas are composite and confused rather than simple, distinct and clear. In order to reason well, we need to find a method that will allow us to distinguish these confused ideas from clear and simple ideas. This method consists of examining the ideas that we have in terms of their logical composition and epistemic origin: Ideas that arise from sensation or the imagination are less clear than ideas that derive directly from reason (epistemic origin). Ideas that involve basic or first principles are clearer than ideas that involve a combination of such first principles (logical composition). Now, the important feature of this method is that the analysis can be conducted, at least initially, within the horizon of one's own ideas. According to Descartes, we can thus judge the truth of each idea according to its own intrinsic features. Descartes subsequently proposes to treat all metaphysical questions from the vantage point of this critical method. He thus formulates a *subjectivist* programme for philosophy.

Spinoza's deductive-genetic method is opposed to this subjectivism, according to Deleuze. Whereas Descartes was mainly concerned with the epistemological question of how one can acquire true ideas, Spinoza's epistemology is mainly concerned with the problem of determining the place that the human mind and its activities occupy within the structure of reality. The elaboration of this problem does not have its beginning in the individual mind or in a subject examining its own mind, but in a description of reality as a whole, as an infinite and all-encompassing substance. The mind is then analysed within the context of this metaphysics of divine substance.

To think genetically from the point of view of a conception of reality as a whole, then, is the ideal contained in the principle of immanence. To think immanently means therefore to strive to articulate in thought as directly as possible the forces of production that produce and govern reality. This genetic principle of immanence will, as we shall see, be the guiding methodological principle also in *Anti-Oedipus* and *A Thousand Plateaus*.

Virtuality, Difference, Sense

One difficulty arising from Spinoza's genetic method is that it cannot properly account for order and relations within reality. Spinoza says that each mode has its own, singular essence, thus opposing the Aristotelian method of classification in which a thing's essence is precisely what it has in common with other things of the same kind, the marks of identity which allow us to situate it at a certain place in reality and in a definite relation to everything else. The genetic method does not proceed by classification, but the problem of order remains. How can it be that the modes produced by substance are not all identical?

Deleuze faced a similar problem in his book on Bergson's spiritual metaphysics of life. In this book, Deleuze reconstructs Bergson's concept of life so that it becomes a process of immanent differentiation, proceeding through separation and composition of layers of reality. These layers are real but they are not physical. In Bergson's spiritualist metaphysics Deleuze thus finds a level of reality that is not given as physical nature without consisting simply in formal principles, like the rules of logic. This level of reality, which Deleuze calls 'virtual', consists of ordering principles that determine reality from within. These conditioning principles are then immanent in reality without nevertheless being an observable part of reality.

The virtual is a level of order which conditions both thought and being. It makes thought possible in so far as thought is a process that requires *order* and hence differentiation. The virtual also makes reality possible as a differentiated field of being. *Difference and Repetition* is an elaborate theory of virtual ordering processes conceived as the immanent genetic principles of reality. *The Logic of Sense* is a theory of virtual ordering processes existing as a border, separating and coordinating thought, language and reality. The two books have the same starting point, the ordering processes that condition thought and reality, but they address different metaphysical problems. The problem analysed in *Difference and Repetition* is how it is possible to produce a genetic account of determination that would escape the system of identification and classification that he calls representation.

The aim of this genetic account is to show that the process which determines something to be what it is, is a genetic virtual principle which at the same time accounts for the thing being different from everything else. However, it accounts for this difference outside any system of classification as pure difference. *The Logic of Sense* constructs a different critique of representation. It goes back to Stoic logic to present a theory of language and thought that will challenge the representationalist, and more specifically *phenomenological*, notion of language as an intentional relation to the world, the notion that language use is defined by an intentional direction, leading from a psychological representation, via a general conceptual content to a physical or ideal referent. This principle of intentionality is opposed to the principle of 'sense'. Sense is a virtual ordering process which makes language possible. Sense does not belong to any particular speaker and does not depend on the referential value of the words used. On the contrary, sense is what makes it possible for individual speakers to produce a meaningful statement referring to a particular object.

The arguments in these two treatises seem, at first, very different. The argument in *Difference and Repetition* concerns ontology, whereas

The Logic of Sense concerns language and thought. But both arguments present a critique of representation from the point of view of
a principle of immanence. The determination of individual beings
must be understood from the inside of a genetic process of determination and not through the mediation of a logical grid of classification. The ordering process that language presupposes must be
understood from within the plane of 'sense' and not with reference
to anything outside of this plane, such as individual speakers or the
world they purport to speak about. I shall discuss each of these two
parallel books in turn.

The Determination of Difference

The argument in *Difference and Repetition* is twofold. On the one
hand, it seeks to show how thought may develop a capacity for
abstraction that will allow it to move beyond representation. On the
other hand, it presents an account of immanent genetic ordering
principles in reality, principles which are not dependent on the
Aristotelian model of logical determination. We will first look at
this second argument concerning genetic determination.

The framework for Deleuze's argument is set by Kant's transcendental philosophy of reason and some of the problems raised within
it. Kant's transcendental philosophy concerns most fundamentally
the grasp that we can have in thought of reality, and by implication,
the nature and scope of 'metaphysics' understood as a purely rational discourse purporting to give a truthful and universally valid
account of reality.

One of the basic principles of Kant's transcendental philosophy
is that we only have access to the world through our own thoughts
and sensory experience. We therefore have no vantage point outside
our own thoughts and judgements from which to judge whether
these are true universally and not just in conformity with the empirical world of phenomena. We cannot judge whether our judgements
are true of the world as it is or would be in itself independently of
how we experience it as a phenomenal world.

The second principle, following on from this, is that a certain
kind of metaphysical knowledge is inaccessible to us in so far as we
are beings who can only know the world from the perspective of
sense experience, i.e. as a phenomenal world stretched out in space
and time. This metaphysical knowledge would be absolute, that is,
non-sensory. It would be the knowledge that a non-sensory intellect

could have. Kant assumes that this kind of knowledge would consist of a complete, that is exhaustive, knowledge of the conditions that determine each thing to be what it is and as it is. This means that for Kant – and in this he differs from Plato's conception of ideal knowledge – one of the marks of metaphysical knowledge is that it consists of a rational grasp of real existing individuals. The individual is known metaphysically when it is known not just as a phenomenon located in space in time, but as a being that underlies a certain range of conditions determining that thing individually, i.e. determining it uniquely and not just in so far as it has to conform to general natural laws.

This ideal of a complete metaphysical knowledge that consists in a knowledge of individuals was not invented by Kant. It had been formulated already by Kant's predecessor Leibniz. One may say that Kant's transcendental philosophy is a response to Leibniz's ideal of a complete knowledge of individual things. Leibniz, for his part, had arrived at his ideal of knowledge through a metaphysical and logical argument. He believed that everything that can be known about something, i.e. all the predicates that can truly be ascribed to a thing must, in some sense, already be included in that thing. This means that predication if it is true is 'analytical': it adds nothing new to the thing, but merely analyses what that thing contains. Knowledge therefore is simply to know all the predicates that are included in each thing.

The metaphysical system corresponding to this conception of knowledge and predication is one in which God, who is omnipotent and omniscient, must know the world that he chooses to create. This means that he must know all that is true of all the beings that make up the world. This means further that he must know all the events that happen to these created beings, since what is true of a created being is what happens to it, the events that fill up its life span. Leibniz thereby arrived at formulating a completely deterministic system in which all events are determined in advance as parts of God's creation. These events are predicates that can be ascribed to individual beings, the spiritual substances or 'monads' that reality consists of in his system. Because, then, all that is true of these monads, the events that make up their life and the predicates that can be ascribed to them, are fixed in advance, each individual thing is completely and exhaustively determined. It is determined in a much deeper and metaphysical sense than it would be according to the Aristotelian principle of determination through identification and classification. For in Leibniz, what is determined is the individual in itself: the individual is determined not just to be a certain kind of thing, but to be this precise being, with this exact life span.

This ideal of exhaustive and real determination of existing individuals is treated by Kant as something that we aspire to think. The knowledge of such an exhaustive determination of individuals has the status of what Kant calls an Idea of reason. The Idea of reason makes us think a determination that we could never know, since in order to know this determination we would have to know reality outside of the conditions of space and time, whereas what we can know are only the phenomena appearing in space and time. The Idea of reason is thus directly wedded to the notion of the individual thing as it is in itself independently of our experience.

Kant had a follower, who is very important to Deleuze, called Salomon Maimon.[10] He was a contemporary of Kant who thought that Kant had gone too far in driving a wedge between our sensory knowledge and experience, and the divine knowledge of individual and real determination, of which we, according to Kant, can only form an Idea of reason. Maimon denied that there was this split between rational and sensory knowledge, but he agreed with Kant that human beings cannot know the world absolutely, i.e. cannot know the exhaustive determination of each individual thing. Nevertheless, it would be wrong to deny that there is what Leibniz called a sufficient reason for each thing, that is an exhaustive determination, determining each thing to be what it is. We can form an Idea of this sufficient reason, but the Idea is not completely separate from our experience of individual objects. Rather, we approach the Idea as a limit of our knowledge. The Idea corresponds directly to a principle of determination, making each individual thing *be* what it is. This principle is the sufficient reason of each thing, its genetic principle. Maimon calls this genetic principle the differential by analogy with the formula expressing the slope of a curve in mathematical calculus. For just as the differential expresses the curve in the sense that it is a sufficient reason for producing it, so the differential idea of each individual thing contains the sufficient genetic cause for producing that thing in its complete determination.

Maimon thereby completes a sort of revolution in modern philosophy, a revolution that started in mathematics with the invention of calculus and Cartesian geometry. This modern mathematics entailed a genetic concept of what it is for an object to be determined, and this genetic concept differed completely from the old Aristotelian model of determination through classification. As this ideal of genetic determination entered philosophy, it first influenced theories of definition and of knowledge. It was thus thought by seventeenth-century philosophers like Hobbes and Spinoza that to know and define an object is to generate it and not to classify it. Now, the deterministic system of Leibniz continues and radicalizes this genetic concept of knowledge by claiming that there is a genetic cause within the mind of God determining each thing to be exactly what it is before it is created. So just as the geometer can generate a figure by knowing its coordinates, God possesses a genetic principle or reason that is sufficient to create each individual being.[11]

Maimon stands at the culmination point of this tradition in that he makes explicit the consequences it has for the tradition of ontology: if determination is genetic and concerns the individual, then the Aristotelian principle of determination through classification is no longer valid. This, at least, is the implication that Deleuze takes from Maimon's philosophy of the differential. *Difference and Repetition* can be seen as tracing a middle path between Kant and Maimon, between Kant's transcendental philosophy of the conditions and limits of thought and Maimon's – and implicitly Leibniz's – philosophy of exhaustive individual determination, conceived independently of how we experience the world (Kant), and independently of any general classification of the world into kinds (Aristotle).

Thus, the two main concepts in *Difference and Repetition*, i.e. the 'problem' and 'determination', each refer to one of these poles of thought. The problem is the object of thought corresponding to our efforts to reach beyond experience and grasp the Ideal determination. Determination is the objective individual cause of each existing thing, the genetic reason that accounts for every being individually, independently of how we may ever get to know this determination.

Within representation, we are only able to grasp individuality and thus difference through the mediation of general contents, such as the concepts of kinds or qualities. Yet if actual individuality is determined genetically along a route that has nothing in common with this adding up of general descriptive predicates, then to know individuality and difference would mean to think in a way that is not dependent on general conceptual contents. This would mean that we would able to think genetically parallel to the process of actual determination in reality. Even if one did not actually know the sufficient reason for each thing, one could approach such a knowledge by finding equivalents in thought for the elements that constitute this genetic process. This exactly is the task that *Difference and Repetition* sets itself: on the one hand, to find a vocabulary that describes the genetic determination in such a way that this process becomes thinkable – although perhaps not knowable in each case – and, on the other, to show how the mind is able to develop a level of abstraction that is sufficient for thinking this process of determination.

According to Deleuze, genetic determination proceeds from a selection on a virtual plane among pairs of 'disjunctive' possibilities – or more properly, 'virtualities'. Deleuze now distinguishes virtuality from the kind of 'possibility' that one finds for instance in the metaphysics of Aristotle under the name 'potentiality' (*dynamis*). This potentiality is stated within the definition of the thing as the potential that is proper to that thing. It is possible for a human being to develop reason, for instance, because it is the essential and defining potential of human beings to be rational. In this case, what is possible is thus also predictable and the future that is possible is already given as a potential in the present.

The 'possibility' of virtual alternatives is very different. Nothing in the present allows us to predict the future. The future is radically open at each instant. For each actualized virtuality, another equally possible virtuality is not realized, and these unrealized virtualities are always given as disjunctive alternatives present within any moment. This means that the present is a site of bifurcation, a moment of choice where the world is moving in one direction rather than another, de-selecting another, equally possible, future world. Within this philosophy of virtual disjunction, the universe is not viewed in its temporal continuity, but rather as a series of instants or short time spans in which each time one of a disjunctive pair is selected. Every instant or short time span thereby throws open the set of constellations that the universe consists of, selecting and realizing new virtualities.

Through this concept of virtual composition and successive, unpredictable actualization Deleuze distances his own philosophy from the determinism and metaphysical rationalism of Spinoza and Leibniz. For the logic of virtual disjunction is consistent neither with the notion of genetic laws residing in a divine nature (Spinoza) nor with the principle of divine foreknowledge of the world's development.

Deleuze thereby preserves a principle of chance and indeterminacy that had featured also in his account of 'will to power' in Nietzsche – there is no rational justification for what the will to power selects – and in his book on Bergson. Deleuze says that Bergson constructs a metaphysics of an irreducibly open-ended universe. This principle is also valid for *Difference and Repetition*.

From Repetition to the Problem

The parallel question to that of determination and virtual composition concerns the relationship between thought and reality. How do thought, and mental activity generally, develop within the cosmos and how does thought develop internal structures that are adequate to understanding virtuality and genetic determination?

Deleuze uses the philosophical concept of 'repetition' as a guiding thread in his presentation of a theory of the mind. He discusses four theories of repetition, those of Hume, Bergson, Freud and Nietzsche: the repetition of habit (Hume), the repetition of memory (Bergson), compulsory repetition (Freud), and the metaphysical theory of the world as a movement of 'eternal recurrence' proposed by Nietzsche. These theories of repetition have in common that repetition in each case presupposes a parallel or accompanying process of mental activity. An activity of synthesis is necessary for an observer to note that the sun rises today *again* (habit). A different kind of synthesis is required to repeat in the mind something that happened *in the past* (memory). It is further only a mind, albeit an unconscious one, that is able to steer, again and again, towards the same *unchosen* action (compulsion). And it is only a mind confronting the totality of life and existence which can conceive of this process as one of *cosmic repetition* (eternal recurrence). If a certain kind of mental activity is thus required in each case, it is not clear that it is one and the same mental activity that is required for all these cases.

There are in Deleuze's account of repetition three dimensions of mental activity corresponding to the present, the past and the future. The present is the life of the mind within a biological context of existence. Deleuze here follows Bergson who argued that philosophy has to understand both how the mind operates within a natural and pragmatic context, and be able to leave this context behind when it seeks to understand the order of reality that the mind is part of. Thus, Bergson says in *Creative Evolution*: 'But these difficulties and contradictions [of speculative philosophy] all arise from trying to apply the usual forms of our thought to objects with which our industry has nothing to do, and for which, therefore, our moulds are not made.'[12]

For Deleuze, our natural 'industry' is manifest at first in a very rudimentary ordering activity, a synthesis of the imagination in which it simply holds together the two poles of a repetitive movement. Already the body exercises such acts of synthesis and imagination in that it is able to connect and hold together sensations and to recognize them when they repeat themselves. At this primary stage of development, the mind derives pleasure from its own activity and from the sensations it holds together in the continuous present of its life, a present which is itself grounded in the continuity of the body's own habits. This stage then constitutes a primary narcissistic level of mental life.

If we now take a step back and look at Deleuze's philosophical method in developing a theory of mental activity, we can see that the concept of repetition fulfils two different strategic functions which are both related to very basic and entrenched problems in modern philosophy.

The first problem that is addressed by repetition is the relationship between physical and mental activity in the development of cognitive faculties. Broadly following Bergson, Deleuze suggests that the mind begins within the biological organism but then develops continuously from this base until it reaches, as we shall see shortly, a level of thought that can only be accounted for as being the product of a mind independent of its location within a body and within a biological environment. The account of the mind thus begins in the body and ends with the presentation of an entirely non-physical, and non-utilitarian mental or 'spiritual' activity. For Deleuze also follows Bergson quite closely in associating utilitarian and practical rationality, the occupation with current problems and objects present within an immediate context of perception, with our most base and basic biological capacities, whereas the emergence of thought is dependent on moving beyond this immediate context of perception and practical need.

The other problem addressed by the concept of repetition is related to the first but is less metaphysical; it does not concern the relation between mind and body but the relation between consciousness and world, between 'subject' and 'object'. The immense strategic advantage and importance of the concept of repetition lie in articulating the development of mental activity and cognitive capability in isolation from any intentional relation to objects. If there is a 'subject' of repetition, it is not transcendental: it is not a centre of representation corresponding to a system of judgement determining objects in the empirical world.

This motive of separating mental activity, thought or language from intentionality is a constant theme in Deleuze's early philosophy. It is weakened in *Anti-Oedipus* and *A Thousand Plateaus* by the concepts of the *machine* and the *rhizome* which imply some kind of relationship between thought and world, but it returns in Deleuze's later work, in his books on Leibniz and on cinema. One may say that Bergson for Deleuze embodies an idealist temptation, the temptation, namely, of a subjective idealism that would equate immanence with the field of mental activity. The materialist Guattari weakened this pull, but it comes back in these last writings on Leibniz and cinema in an aesthetic form.

Returning to the genetic account of the mind in *Difference and Repetition*, the second level of mental activity introduces a break with the first, in that the first marks an unbroken relation to the world that is present to the senses. On the primary narcissistic level the mind is not able to think non-being or absence and it is therefore also not able to think relations and difference. For the mind to break with this closed sphere of a continuous present, it has to open up to the past, not simply the past seen from the point of view of the present, but the past as an independent region of being that can only be reached by moving beyond the sphere of the immediate present of perception.

There is a relation to the past which Deleuze calls 'pure memory', in which the past is revealed as a *virtual realm of being*. The kind of memory that is able to disclose this virtual region of the past is sharply distinct from the mental activities of perception and awareness that are oriented towards the present. Following Bergson's analysis of memory as being entirely distinct from perception and involving a completely different structure of mental activity, Deleuze thus argues that memory in its purest form introduces the mind not only to a different realm of being – the virtual past – but also to a different dimension of thought. This is a realm of thought consisting of formal operations of combination, and of abstract relations of difference. These combinations and relations can only be thought of the primary sphere of the present in which we of course only grasp and relate to what is actually present before us.

This theory of virtual being further means that the present moment is itself as if split, composed internally and virtually of two temporal dimensions, on the one hand, a present tense – *this is now* – and, on the other, *a movement of passing away*. This movement of passing away is for the present already *to belong to the past* at the moment of being taken up by it, otherwise the present and the past would be cut off from one another. The present is thus virtually both present (first synthesis) and passing away (second synthesis). The second synthesis is then the capacity to synthesize the present with the past and from the point of view of the past. For thought, this means that mental activity in the second synthesis moves beyond the mere recording of what takes place before it.

By opening up to virtuality, the mind is now able to conceive of parallel series virtually co-existing in the same present. Deleuze finds this notion of virtually parallel series developed in modern fiction, for instance, in the philosophical tales of the Argentinean writer Jorge Luis Borges. Thus, Borges tells a story where the possibilities of the narrative are not realized one at a time, so that the ones that are realized exclude the ones that are not realized. Instead, all the possibilities of the narrative co-exist as a virtual composition.

From primary narcissism to virtual complexity – this arc corresponds to a move from perception to thought. Perception arises out of the first synthesis of biological habit; thought is made possible by the virtual complexity of the second synthesis. Deleuze compares the duality of first and second synthesis with Kant's concepts of experience composed of sensibility and understanding. For Kant, sensibility and understanding exhaustively describe the field of experience but Kant also states that a part of our thinking, speculative reason, cannot find its objects – the self, the world as a whole, God – within experience as there is a sharp split in Kant's system between experience and speculative thought. This is not so for Deleuze. He identifies a *third synthesis*, a third dimension of mental activity which goes beyond the first two syntheses but which is nevertheless not cut off from reality. This third synthesis is the synthesis of *abstraction*, which is the condition for philosophical thought. Deleuze argues that it is only when the mind goes beyond what is given to it in experience that it is able to realize its potential for thought. This process begins but is not completed with the second synthesis which is still embedded in a natural context of experience, namely, the 'rememberer's' own past experience.

The third synthesis of abstraction has four characteristics: (1) it is related to the *future*; (2) it is purely *abstract*; (3) it is conditioned by an *interruption* of the vital instincts of habit; and (4) it depends on a special kind of *receptivity*.

It is only if the mind is receptive in a certain way that it can move beyond its natural and biological drive towards grasping what is given in perception or memory. This move beyond the given constitutes an *ascesis* of thought. This ascesis is articulated in Freudian terms. Deleuze combines terms from two stages of psychoanalytic theory: the theory of narcissism which leads to the distinction between the ego and the super-ego, and the later concept of the death-drive. Narcissism is a withdrawal of sexual or 'libidinal' energy from its normal orientation towards external objects. This energy is now invested in an internal object, an idealized version of the person's own self, an ideal ego functioning as an internalized figure of moral authority. The death-drive, or Thanatos, marks a more radical break with the libido. It operates outside of and independently of the libidinal drives. The libidinal drives function according to a simple 'principle of pleasure': they push towards a release from tension and unrest. The death-drive functions on a deeper level as a pull towards a more fundamental rest and stasis achieved through a return to inanimate matter.

Both narcissism and Thanatos thus imply a break with the circuit of vital energy, the former in the figure of abstraction and interiority that is the moral ego, the second in a movement of return to a previous stage of being. Both these ideas, the construction of an internal abstraction detached from vital energy and the idea of a return to a previous stage of reality, find a deep resonance in Deleuze's thought. They are fused into the concept of a 'body without organs', a notion originally used by the experimental playwright Antonin Artaud in the context of a critique of individual psychology. In *A Thousand Plateaus*, this notion of a body without organs will become an important ethical term, the idea being that we can only escape social and political oppression by undoing the effects of social and political forces in ourselves. This would mean undoing our social self or personality in order to return to a prior state of being, reaching the organized level of life which is the 'body without organs'.

In *Difference and Repetition*, the emphasis and the argument are different. The break with libido energy serves to articulate the conditions of abstract thought. We can only become autonomous as thinking beings if we can undergo a radical ascesis allowing us to form within ourselves a plane of abstraction that is the body without organs. This level of abstraction is characterized by a more definitive separation of our combinatory capability from practical needs than what was possible in the second synthesis of memory. This separation is presented by Deleuze in temporal terms, as the capacity to separate time as a condition of experience from the order of succession that we encounter *in* experience:

It is not a question of acquiring thought, nor of exercising it as though it were innate, but of engendering the act of thinking within thought itself, perhaps under the influence of a violence which causes the reflux of libido on to the narcissistic ego, and in the same movement both extracting Thanatos from Eros and abstracting time from all content in order to separate out the pure form.[13]

Thought moves beyond the rational model of representation by purifying itself from the contents of perception and pragmatic needs, thus purifying itself as abstraction. Thinking, then, is for Deleuze something that we *undergo* rather than simply something that we *do*. We may ask: why is it the body rather than the mind that is involved in the third synthesis? Because the move beyond the present and the real towards pure abstraction is a process that affects the body as much as the mind. For it is through the body and its repetitions that I am anchored in the present of primary narcissism.

The relation to the world that culminates in this ascesis is one of *problematization*. Thought is not a representation of what is given and actual but a continuous problematization. A problem is a thought-object that is never identical with a fact or a thing, but any situation, even the most basic, may pose a problem; it may put us before a problem that we therefore have not simply invented, but which nevertheless requires a certain response in order to manifest itself. This response is the basic capacity for thought. It arises within the primary synthesis as the grasping of something being the sign for something else. When the imagination holds together the idea of clouds and the idea that it may rain, it forms out of the idea of the cloud, a sign. The sign is not identical with the cloud, but the cloud seen, or rather problematized in a certain way. The second synthesis is able to pose much more complex problems, arising from the correlation of series that are not grounded in the same causal chain. The third synthesis liberates the problem as an exploration of relations in thought unconstrained by any empirical content.

The Sayable and the Thinkable

The Logic of Sense conducts a parallel argument to the genetic theory of *Difference and Repetition*. It is an account of the relation between language, thought and world formulated in opposition to the phenomenological concept of 'intentionality' or conscious directedness.

Instead of seeing mind, language and world as coordinated by conscious acts, moving towards the world through the mediation of a mental and conceptual 'content', this relationship is conceived from the external and ontological point of view of an ideal border separating and coordinating what is sayable and thinkable with the world. This border does not depend on any act of consciousness, or subjective experience. Yet it is also different from a merely formal, structuralist or semiotic system, as we shall see.

Thought is again seen to emerge from reality, but this time not so much in so far as it is a certain kind of activity but rather because the content of thought, the *thinkable*, has its own reality; it is an *ideal or logical surface of the world*. On this surface thought encounters the world through language, relations are formed and the linguistic operations required by speech are made possible. The surface is real – it has a certain mode of being, related to the being of the world – but it is at the same time distinct both from the world and from the mind.

Representation articulates thought with reference to individual objects. The representational conception of language conceives of speech as a threefold relation between an individual speaker, a state of affairs that is referred to and a conceptual content or signification through which objects and their properties are identified. This view of language rests on certain metaphysical assumptions. It supposes, first, that before language is used by any individual speaker, such speakers and a world of individual objects are already given as a structure within reality. Second, this view takes for granted, following on from this idea, that words and their meanings serve to connect these two types of individuals, the individual speaker and the individual object in the world. Language is, then, on this view, a tool allowing us to orient ourselves in the world and to communicate contents about items in the world to others. Deleuze does not assume that these individual entities are given as primary beings. *Difference and Repetition* argues that the term 'individual' refers to the actualization of difference within a 'field of individuation', and not to something like classifiable objects. Here, similarly, Deleuze does not take the signifying capacity of language to depend on any such fixed individuals. He conceives of the relationship between the three dimensions of language, the speaker, the referent and the meaning as three linguistic functions, which he calls manifestation (speaker), designation (referent) and signification (meaning). His question is now how these functions are organized in relation to one another.

In the representational model they directly correspond to each other as they are situated on an axis of intentionality, leading from the mind to the world. The proposition 'This is a tree' is first a *mental representation*; then it involves the use of the *concept* 'tree' to identify an individual object of perception as the *referent* of the proposition.

Deleuze's philosophy of language is opposed to this model because it makes language use dependent on perception. He argues instead that the three linguistic functions are organized immanently on the surface of sense independently of the use of language in communication. Sense is thus not only a sphere of coordination between these linguistic functions but also the generative principle which first produces them. Sense is thus a structural and genetic totality producing the functions that it contains. The three functions of manifestation, designation and signification constitute three aspects of what makes an utterance meaningful. The utterance carries meaning because someone utters it, because it is about something and because the words themselves have meaning, but none of these functions can operate on their own. They depend on the fourth dimension of sense. For it is only on the level of sense that something can appear as meaningful in the first place, before being uttered, being about something, carrying a signification. This primary level of sense is at the same time what introduces thought into language. For sense is the logical medium of what can be said and thought. It is the medium of all the relations that can be formed in thought and then said. These relations constitute, we may say, what is sayable and thinkable; they form the primary content of language and the mind.

This logical medium has a similar ontological status to that of the virtual composition of time in *Difference and Repetition*. It is neither completely formal like mathematics nor a psychological feature of how we think nor is it derived from experience. Sense constitutes the possible objects of thought before we enter thought, before we have any concrete thoughts about any specific object. For the objects of thought are at first constituted by what is thinkable. The thinkable is the total set of abstract relations that can be formed. This genetic principle of a surface of sense giving to thought its possible objects has an ambiguous metaphysical status. For the border separating thought and language from the physical world also co-ordinates them. It is only on this surface of sense that it is possible to articulate relations of difference and order. In what sense therefore can one say that relations exist in the world independently of this surface of sense? This question raises the possibility of a kind of Idealism in which the world itself would be produced by sense. This is a possibility that is also envisaged in Deleuze's text:

> It appears that sense, in its organization of aleatory and singular points, problems and questions, series and displacements, is doubly generative: not only does it engender the logical proposition with its determinate dimensions (designation, manifestation, and significa-tion); it engenders also the objective correlates of this proposition which were themselves first produced as ontological propositions (the designated, the manifested, and the signified).[14]

The idealism envisaged here is objective rather than subjective; it is not an idealism that consists in separating a mental realm from its intentional correlates in the world, as we saw a move towards in *Difference and Repetition*. This is a more Platonic scenario in which the articulation of the world as a differentiated totality would be dependent on a formal and ideal structure, which in turn would not be derived from anything existing in the world. Deleuze does not pursue this idealist line of thinking. In *The Logic of Sense*, he is concerned most of all to emphasize that the relations that we observe in perception and articulate in thought and language have an origin that is different from language, thought and perception, an origin which in itself is neutral with respect to conventional logical dis-tinctions. The notion of the neutral taken from Blanchot entails a concept of 'inhumanity', of a dimension of reality that is indifferent to our human, pragmatic and existential, concerns: 'In relation to propositional modes in general, the neutrality of sense appears from several different perspectives. From the point of view of quan-tity, sense is neither particular nor general, neither universal nor personal. From the point of view of quality, it is entirely indepen-dent of both affirmation and negation.'[15]

I said in the Introduction that Blanchot's concept of the neutral is important to Deleuze because it allows him to gain an 'inhuman' and non-subjective perspective upon human life. In *The Logic of Sense*, he moves on to use this perspective, developed in the theory of sense, to construct an *ethics*, a philosophy of life seen from a point of view that is outside of ordinary human experience. This passage from language via logic to ethics is facilitated in Deleuze's text by its reliance on Stoic philosophy. For the Stoics also conceived of philosophy as falling into distinct parts – physics, logic, ethics – which were ultimately coordinated.

The notion of sense as what can be said is itself the development of a Stoic concept, the concept of the *lekton*, usually translated as the 'sayable'. In a famous fragment the Stoics are reported as making a distinction between three elements of language: the sound or utterance, something referred to and which can be perceived, and, finally, a third element, which is not, like sound or a thing, something physical, but the state of affairs that the utterance claims to be the case.

In defining thought, the Stoics claimed that truth and falsehood are ascribed to what they called 'signification', but they held this signification to depend on a relationship between three things:

> 'the signification, 'the signifier', and 'the name-bearer'. The signifier is an utterance [sound], for instance 'Dion'; the signification is the actual state of affairs revealed by an utterance, and which we apprehend as it subsists in accordance with our thought . . . the name-bearer is the external object, for instance Dion himself. Of these, two are bodies – the utterance and the name-bearer; but one is incorporeal – the state of affairs signified and sayable, which is true or false.[16]

By defining 'the state of affairs' as incorporeal or non-physical, the Stoics make the claim that language and thought cannot simply relate to the world directly, as if enumerating or listing things. Thought always establishes relations, for instance, of causality, and these relations are not observable and physical in the same way that things are. Now, at the same time this incorporeal sphere of what can be thought and said is itself real. This is the Stoic principle that Deleuze develops further in *The Logic of Sense*.

The Stoics developed the theory of the sayable through an original, cosmological theory of causes and of causal determination. They distinguished between two kinds of causality. The universe as a whole is one all-encompassing system of interacting causes. This order of causality is beyond our grasp. By contrast, the predicates that we ascribe to things in ordinary language use and the causes we perceive in experience do not correspond to this all-encompassing order. The predicates do not grasp the place of the thing in the order of the universe and the cause we identify in experience is only a quasi-cause, divorced from the actual moving cause behind the event within the order of the cosmos.

Millman?

Deleuze borrows this distinction and combines it with his own theory of destiny conceived as a virtual composition or causes. According to this theory, our life, the life that we actualize, is a variation and repetition of the composition of causes that we virtually are. This relationship of destiny between virtual composition and actual variation-repetition does not correspond to the linear and sequential order of experience. For within the order of experience, the events that make up my life have a determined location in time and determined causes attached to them. *After* the event A and *because of* event B, event C happened. This is how we represent our lives to ourselves. Yet this linear order of time and causality has a merely discursive or linguistic reality. The causes and predicates that we thereby name do not actually refer to any real causal process. For the actual causal process that characterizes our lives is *genetic* and *compositional*, an inner, and therefore not *empirical* causality. A person is a virtual and genetic composition of potentialities that express themselves through repetition and variation. The events that form the content of a person's life are the expressions of this repetition and variation.

Within this genetic order of expression, the event is not located within the linear time of representation. If we were able to think the event on this genetic level, it would appear detached also from its immediate causal context, the web of 'quasi-causes' that we attribute to events within representation and within conscious experience.

In so far as my life can do nothing but continue this repetition-variation, we may also say that this pattern of repetition and variation constitutes a kind of fate or destiny. In that sense the event becomes almost inseparable from destiny. Each event is a particular expression of the total variation-repetition of virtualities that compose my being.

This neo-Stoic conception of destiny is also the starting point for Deleuze's conception of literature. Literature is able to embody these virtual relations and the compositions between them far better than we normally can do in thought or in ordinary language. It is therefore a natural next step to look at Deleuze's theory of literature before turning to the political philosophy he developed in collaboration with Félix Guattari. In fact, it will turn out that it is within the domain of literary criticism that Deleuze moves from the metaphysical and genetic philosophy of *Difference and Repetition* and *The Logic of Sense* towards a new type of philosophy centred on the concept of the *sign*.

It is through the exploration of the problem of signs and signification that Deleuze is able to create a bridge between his earlier
metaphysical system and the political concerns and debate with the
social sciences that he comes to share with Guattari. The next chapter charts this transition from metaphysics to political theory and
the epistemology of social science, by studying Deleuze's theory
of signs.

2

Cultural Semiotics

Literature and the Logic of Sense

There are two competing strands in Deleuze's work from the late 1960s onwards. One is ontological. It is an effort to formulate a general theory of production and genetic processes. The other is transcendental and consists in analysing the relations from which language and thought as well as any social or cultural practice are formed.

The Logic of Sense, which analyses the transcendental conditions of thought and language, combines these strands and provides an ontological theory of sense. On the basis of this ontology, literature can be conceptualized as the expression of a logic of sense, hence as embodied thought. A particular work of literature would thus be the expression of a particular set of sense relations, constituting a particular thought form.

At the general ontological level of sense, the logic of sense is the embodiment of thought forms upon the immaterial surface of sense. Literature, and modernist narrative literature in particular, is then a specific articulation of these thought forms. As the thought forms on the surface of sense also fulfil a transcendental function – presenting the basic relations through which it is possible to think about the world – a work of literature also presents a particular thought form identifying a particular set of formal relations.

These formal relations organize time, body, language and action within the literary text. Through the organizing effect of these formal relations the text is able to present a particular perspective on human life. The modernist narrative literature that is of primary interest to Deleuze is able to present a perspective on human life that differs from and even challenges the perspective on the world that we have within everyday experience. Literary modernity thus not only challenges nineteenth-century narrative or realist conventions, it also challenges experience itself. It presents perspectives on life and on ourselves as beings of desire, living in time, using language and interacting physically with the world and these perspectives are not coordinated by pragmatic and ordinary practical concerns or by self-conscious experience.

Deleuze therefore views modernist narrative literature as capable of posing *ethical* and *metaphysical* problems in that it can express a non-anthropocentric or anti-humanist point of view upon subjective experience. This viewpoint corresponds not only to a 'logic of sense' but also to Deleuze's own conceptions of time, life and destiny in which the time of an individual life is not seen as a linear, progressive sequence, but as a structure of repetition and variation.

The texts of Deleuze's favourite writers, such as Fitzgerald, Gombrowicz or Klossowski produce narratives composed according to principles other than those of plot, character and action. These conventional narrative principles all presuppose a notion of *intentional action* as the causal drive of the story. By composing the content of narrative in a way that sidesteps intentionality or makes it seem subordinate to other ordering principles, these writers therefore attain a perspective on human life that is not that of action or pragmatic subjectivity. In Fitzgerald, this is the perspective of destiny; in Gombrowicz, it is the strange doubling of characters and events and the underlying tone of sexual tension that cannot be located in any one of them; in Klossowski, it is a theological eroticism in which perversion and Satanism combine to form actions that appear inevitable within a certain structure of desire – but this desire itself remains enigmatic.

Literature thereby presents alternatives to the concept of the self-conscious subject as a centre of coordination within experience. In *Difference and Repetition*, Deleuze himself presents such an alternative subject which he calls the 'embryonic subject' (*le sujet larvaire*). This 'subject' is 'the person who I am' in so far as I *undergo a process* which develops my mental activities and my relation to the world in a certain way. In *The Logic of Sense*, Deleuze continues this elaboration of an alternative subject conception by opposing the phenomenological concept of the world as the horizon of my experience to a logical or 'serial' concept of the world as that set of events that co-exists with any particular event. The subject corresponding to this world is, as we saw, a composition of virtual potentials expressed in the events that make up a person's life and in the repetition and variation of 'themes' that constitute its 'destiny'. If we combine these two concepts of composition and the embryonic subject, we arrive at the notion of the world as a virtual composition of which the embryonic subject is a part, as one composition within another. In this compositional metaphysics life is not viewed from the perspective of conscious, subjective experience but from that of an external, cosmological standpoint. This external point of view is exactly the perspective presented by the twentieth-century experimental novel, according to Deleuze.

Literature thus embodies philosophical ideas. A literary text may also embody a theory of its own status and functioning as literature. Deleuze thus views literary texts as theorizing their own mode of signification. Literary texts are even seen to anticipate and contribute to his own semiotic enquiry. Deleuze's studies in semiotics pursue a twofold aim: one is constructive and the other critical. On the constructive side, semiotics will be a means to find a middle ground between the two conventional philosophical positions of idealism and materialism: the sign and its signification will be theorized as being neither fully material nor straightforwardly ideal.

On the critical side, this search for a middle ground in turn will help Deleuze to formulate an alternative to the concept of the subject in his account of human experience. In semiotic terms it may be possible to describe the structure of experience, society, cognition and culture on the level of sense and signification rather than with reference to a subjective point of view.

Deleuze seeks to do this without, on the other hand, simply replacing the subjective point of view with positivism, i.e. with a scientific explanatory paradigm, reducing experience, cognition, culture, etc. to so-called 'underlying material causes'. The semiotic account is non-reductive; it seeks to maintain and respect the reality of sense within all aspects of human and social reality. The critical dimension of semiotics for Deleuze amounts then to a critique of 'representation' – for subjectivity and positivism are but two faces of representation: the subject is the self-conscious centre of representation; positivism is the view that reality can be represented as a totality of so-called 'facts'. Now this double attack on representation, scientific and subjective, Deleuze finds to be undertaken within literature itself. Thus, what he calls the 'objective illusion', which is a particular version of 'representation', he sees as the central concern of Marcel Proust's novel, *A la recherche du temps perdu* (1913–27).

Proust and the Objective Illusion

In Deleuze's essay on Proust published in its first version in 1964, we find a sustained and complex discussion of the problem representation as this problem is seen to be theorized within the novel itself. The title of his essay, *Proust and Signs* (1964)[1] must therefore be taken in a theoretical sense: this is not a study of signs in Proust's novel, *A la recherche du temps perdu*, but a discursive development of the theoretical problem that the novel unfolds narratively.

The essay thus presents two different sides. It is a work of philosophy, a study in the relationship between thought and signs. It is a work of literary interpretation and a contribution to the scholarship on Proust. These two sides depend on one another. The book radically changed how Proust was read in France but it could only do so because it arrived at a new vantage point from which to analyse a literary work of art as embodied thought.

The reading covers the principal themes of the novel, what any reader of Proust would think about – snobbery, jealousy, time, art – but Deleuze organizes these themes according to a philosophical problem that is not immediately visible on the surface of the text. This problem concerns the nature of signification, the relationship between signification and time and the primary role of art in expressing certain kinds of signification. In developing this problem Deleuze first has to confront the dominant reading of the novel, based on the novel's own, internal theory of memory.

The novel, *A la recherche du temps perdu*, is structured as a frame narrative. A middle-aged man narrates how he came to remember his past in a particular way. The main body of the novel consists of these memories, beginning with the narrator's early childhood and passing through adolescence and youth to the point when he reaches maturity and begins writing the novel that is *A la recherche du temps perdu*. The thread through the story of the narrator's life is thus the question of how he will become the writer of the book *A la recherche du temps perdu*. Within this fiction within the fiction about how the novel was written, a particular kind of experience plays a key role. The narrator has a series of sudden flashes of memory that seem to transport him back directly into the past in a much more powerful way than if he had tried to remember anything from the past *at will*.

Proust calls this kind of memory 'involuntary memory'. Involuntary memory is supposed to give the narrator a particular and privileged access to his own life. With this psychological and aesthetic theory, Proust legitimizes his own art and the position of his narrator.

In much of the secondary literature on Proust the frame narrative and the theory of memory have been key to interpretations of the text. Deleuze contests this principle of interpretation by focusing on the actual temporal unfolding of the story that is told *within the frame narrative*. Through this narrative and temporal unfolding, *A la recherche du temps perdu* demonstrates a capacity to render time in a non-linear way. Showing characters at different points in their lives and from different angles, Proust breaks with a conventional principle of narrative continuity. Deleuze reads this principle of discontinuity as a presentation of *temporal complexity*. Thus, the time of a life is not linear and successive, but different lines of development, different aspects of a personality always co-exist. They are 'complicated' or 'folded' within the person. This non-linear temporality is not derived from the introspective representations of *memory*, nor from the narrator's experiences in the frame narrative. On the contrary, the novel stresses that the narrator has to go through an apprenticeship in life in order to understand the order of time. This apprenticeship passes through different stages which are all concerned with a particular type of *sign*, the signs of love, of social exchange, of time, and of art. Ultimately, this apprenticeship culminates in the narrator becoming a writer, but this involves overcoming a fundamental illusion that is common to all types of signs when we interpret them from the point of view of experience.

Deleuze calls this *the objective illusion*. It consists in confusing the meaning of the sign with the object that it appears to represent. The lover believes that 'the amorous gesture refers to the person that produced it'. The guest at a party thinks that the social exchange he has witnessed communicated real emotion. The subject of memory would like to believe that memory is controlled by a definite past moment or experience. The art lover hopes that art is an ideal mirror and representation of life. Yet in each case the logic of the sign is more complex than that of a simple representation. The sign carries meaning because it composes and develops content independently of what the sign refers to. Love, social exchange, time and art are all dependent on an experience of signs, but these signs are not themselves derived from any experience. This is why the signs of art are the highest form of signification within this semiotic theory that Deleuze ascribes to Proust. For only art, and the art of the novel in particular, can capture this autonomous logic of the sign. The ultimate aim of the art that is the novel, *A la recherche du temps perdu*, is then to present the temporal and virtual complexity of signs and of life.

The Sign, the Subject and Power

The treatises *Anti-Oedipus* and *A Thousand Plateaus* pursue the opposition between *subjectivism* and a *genetic* method on the level of a theory of signification. This theory of signification is itself guided by genetic principles.

Saussure's theory of the sign introduced, as we saw, a rigorous distinction between *signification* within language (based on the differential value of the sign within the language system), and the intended meaning of an utterance and the referential function of the uttered sentence belonging to the sphere of speech (*parole*). This immanence of language as an order of mutually defining terms demarcates an ideal space of meaning where the sign joins a signifier to a signified, thereby producing signification. Deleuze attacks this semiotic idealism, but not in the first instance by stressing the importance of communication – that becomes the argument of Deleuze and Guattari in *A Thousand Plateaus*, where they propose an original theory of linguistic communication. In the 1960s, Deleuze approaches semiotics from a metaphysical perspective, and more specifically through his reading of Spinoza.

In *Spinoza and the Problem of Expression* (1968),[2] Deleuze proposes an original triadic theory of *expression* opposed to the dualistic theory of the signifier and the signified. In Spinoza's metaphysics, the *attribute* expresses the *essence* (i.e. the power) of divine *substance*. In this relationship of expression the essence, or that which is expressed, is not identical to a content (meaning, intention, signified) nor is the essence a thing: the power of substance is neither identical to substance (a thing) nor is it the 'content' or 'meaning' of substance. This notion, the *expressed* as distinct from the object referred to, corresponds on the other hand structurally to Deleuze's own neo-Stoic ontology of sense. The concept of sense is also different both from the world of physical objects and from particular contents or meanings. It constitutes the logical realm of what is sayable and thinkable and which is derived neither from experience nor from the physical order of the world.[3]

This triadic concept of expression contains an argument for the immanence of language that is more subtle than the dualistic idealism of Saussure. For the order of sense, of the thinkable, of the expressed essences, is always dependent on the bearer of the essence, or, in other words, on the reality that language ultimately addresses, the substance in Spinoza or the real order of causes in the Stoics. The sayable is for the Stoics, as we saw, an incorporeal reality. This incorporeal reality is opposed to the corporeal reality of the 'cosmos' composed of bodies in interaction. To claim that sense is *in*corporeal therefore also means that it is relative to or dependent on something else *which is corporeal*.

This relativity of sense, its dependence upon a different, corporeal level of reality, has deep metaphysical and semiotic implications. For it means that the immanence of language is never complete. The semiotic account of language cannot be idealistic in the manner of Saussure. Language does not constitute an entirely self-sufficient realm.

This non-idealism further constitutes a crucial methodological and metaphysical difference between Deleuze, on the one hand, and Lacan and Derrida, on the other – two other thinkers who are sometimes labelled together with Deleuze as 'post-structuralist'. They see language as inhabiting a self-sufficient immaterial realm, governed by internal principles of organization. For Deleuze, by contrast, the immanence of language is always relative to a material world of which it is the surface.

However, the triadic principle also means that Deleuze in his early phase is far from being a pure philosophical materialist. A materialist will try to say that thought or culture, or anything that appears to possess an autonomous and immaterial status, is in fact derived from and caused by material structures or processes, whether physical or economic. Deleuze in his early thought does not accept this materialist thesis of derivation or causation, but affirms on the contrary that thought or culture has a structural autonomy as an immanent genetic order (the serial order of sense). At the same time, however, he conceives of this genetic order as dependent on a physical reality outside of it. Sense is thus paradoxically both autonomous and dependent.

Now a shift of emphasis occurred in Deleuze's thinking arising from his meeting with Félix Guattari. For the latter is concerned to articulate relations of *power* from a psychoanalytic perspective, in terms of desire. Thus, using psychoanalysis to analyse politics also has a reverse effect on their conception of psychoanalysis.

Within this political context they articulate a new psychoanalytic theory founded upon materialist principles: desire is then itself conceived in relation to political power. Through his collaboration with Guattari, Deleuze moves closer to materialism in that he comes to see the realm of sense not only as dependent on the corporeal world, but also as generated by material processes.

The emphasis of the theory of sense that they develop together is nevertheless different from that of a more purely materialist philosopher such as Marx. For Marx, the question was how to accommodate consciousness and culture within a system that is basically socio-economic, thereby defining beliefs and actions in terms of class relations (for instance, higher and lower bourgeoisie) and mode of production (typically, feudalism versus capitalism). The problem that emerges for Deleuze through his collaboration with Guattari is very different. It is a question of how his genetic method can be used to explain the surface of sense within a political framework. In other words, the problem for Deleuze will be to account for the genesis of the thinkable within a given political context, where the thinkable is itself identical with a certain social reality.

This completely new account of social reality as comprising our social categories and the content of cultural practices as a surface of sayables and thinkables differs both from the Marxist theory of ideology and from cultural semiotics. For the socially existing sayable is not simply, as in the theory of ideology, an erroneous representation of reality, a distortion: the socially existing sayable *is* reality in a certain form of expression.

Nor are sayables and thinkables derived from semiotic cultural systems of signification such as texts or images. The surface of sense constitutes a specific ontological layer, a level of reality much deeper than any such particular medium of signification.

This semiotic theory allows Deleuze and Guattari to take seriously the claims made by the human and social sciences amounting to a recognition of a sphere of 'symbolic' reality holding society together. But they provide a completely new account of this 'symbolic' reality that is non-reductive, i.e. it does not seek to reduce this symbolic reality to something else, but, precisely because this account is non-reductive, what it describes is no longer symbolic or signifying, but expressive: the expression of reality as sense.

In the semiotic theory of *Anti-Oedipus*, sense is an ontological realm engendered in social reality through the interaction of two material forces, originating in the psyche and in political power. These two forces are called 'desiring production' and 'social production'. Through their interaction they produce a social level of sense, constituting what is politically and socially thinkable. In order to stress that this social level of sense is both politically engendered by a material process and that it, nevertheless, possesses its own autonomous signifying reality, Deleuze and Guattari call this level of social sense, the *surface of inscription*. Inscription indicates, on the one hand, a material process of inscribing, and, on the other, the reality of a signifying object, i.e. that which has been inscribed.

In this theory, political power is the ability to inscribe what is thinkable upon the social surface of inscription, but power can only operate as inscription through the collaboration of desire. It is thus through the encounter between desire and power that sense is inscribed. This inscriptive encounter is part of a history of political systems. Since power is manifest through inscription, this history is also a semiotic history, that is a history both of the political categories inscribed and of the signifying effect of these categories within social and political reality. Universal political history is thus a history of shifting modes of signification, or 'semiotic regimes'. The semiotic regime now has a particular relation to sexual desire. For it is by interacting with the mass of sexual desire within a society that power becomes inscriptive, but this also means that the surface of inscription in each semiotic regime will entertain a specific relation to desire. This relationship is now theorized by the crucial but very difficult concepts of 'code' and 'codification'.

This term is taken from linguistics where it indicates a set of rules that enable speakers to communicate. The idea of a code is that it is absolutely formal and thus governs all speech and every speaker. However, the French word 'code' also means law, for instance in the expression 'the Napoleonic Code'. In *Anti-Oedipus*, the verb 'to codify' means to spell out in a formal way the implicit rules of a social practice. Deleuze and Guattari also bring a third meaning to the term by associating the abstract character of this formal operation with the abstract quality of money entailed by the Marxist concept of 'surplus value'. In Marxist economic theory, the capitalist derives from industrial production an economic gain, a surplus value, but he fails to return this gain to the workers who produced this value through their labour. He withdraws surplus value in order to reinvest it, thereby allowing a concrete monetary gain to come into circulation and become 'capital', i.e. money available for reinvestment and which is not tied to any concrete property or process of production.

The withdrawal of surplus value is thus a moment in the generation of the abstract reality that is capital. This process of abstraction
is retained by Deleuze and Guattari when they speak of a 'surplus
value of code'. Surplus value of code should not be understood as
involving an excess of codification, but rather a kind of abstract
reality very much like economic surplus value, and consisting of
socially produced sense. The surplus value of code is therefore
nothing other than the social reality of sense; it is a surface of
socially produced thought that has been withdrawn from the immediate consumption of energy within society.

We thus come back to the link observed in *Difference and Repetition* between thought and *ascesis* or the interruption of a circuit of
energy. Just as the ability to generate abstract thought was dependent on the withdrawal of energy from life and the creation of a
'body without organs', so the socially embodied thought, i.e. the
surplus value of code, implies a storing up of social energy. This
genetic semiotics is thus also a philosophy of energy, of energy
being transformed into socially embodied thoughts and systems of
signification.

Politically, the constant collaboration of two types of energy,
power and sexuality, in the production of sense entails that the
social representations of power can never be explained in terms of
a particular direction of dominance. Desire and power are inter-
locked in one social machine. Deleuze and Guattari use the term
machine, social machines and desiring machines, in order to designate this character of socio-sexual energy: it flows through social
relations that organize power in certain ways, but power itself has
no centre and no reality outside of these flows, outside of this functioning.[4] Power in itself is completely alien to representation. It is
not identical to any idea of power. It is not what the King has or
what his subjects endorse or grudgingly accept. It is a social energy
that permeates society.

This view of power is similar to the analysis of discipline in the
works of Michel Foucault, but *Anti-Oedipus* pre-dates Foucault's
book on prison, *Discipline and Punish* (*Surveiller et punir*), by a few
years. So rather than speak of influence we should see Deleuze and
Guattari as working in parallel with Foucault and reaching similar
conclusions. In their sequel to *Anti-Oedipus*, the treatise *A Thousand
Plateaus*, Deleuze and Guattari view Foucault as one of the great
social theorists. Another is the writer Franz Kafka.

The discussion of social semiotics thus brings us back to literature but now with a slightly different, political rather than ethical,

perspective. Kafka is, for Deleuze and Guattari, the most accurate social theorist, but in their book on his life and works they also see him, as Deleuze had seen Proust, as the inventor of his own signifying system or *semiotic regime.*

Kafka's Semiotic Machine

The book, *Kafka: Toward a Minor Literature*, is a programmatic text by Deleuze and Guattari, a text in which they enact an immanent method within a well-defined and circumscribed field, namely the life and works of the writer Franz Kafka. Deleuze and Guattari here present a 'semiotic regime' or organizing principle of signification, governing Kafka's texts in such a way that it encompasses their context of production, Kafka's biography, the narrative structure of his texts and his use of the German language. This semiotic regime can be said to form a *machine*. A machine is defined in this work as a parallel movement of desire and signification which is completely self-sufficient. Nothing outside of the machine needs to be invoked in order to explain how the machine works. A machine is thus a perfectly immanent process.

Each element in the Kafka machine, the components of his stories, their language, their biographical and political context of production, obey the same principle of movement and signification which constitute the logic or mode of functioning of the machine. In the machine there is no primary distinction between signifier and signified, form and content, inside and outside, desire and its object. The logic of the machine is constituted instead by a principle of connectivity that is neutral in relation to these distinctions: the machine in its movement of desire and signification operates by establishing connections.

They arrive at the principle of *semiotic immanence* by applying concepts from the linguistic theory of Louis Hjelmslev. In his theory of signification, Hjelmslev started from Saussure's distinction between 'signifier' and 'signified' which he then sought to refine. He found Saussure's distinction too idealistic and not sufficiently formal. To this end, he introduced the new terms *form of content* and *form of expression.* Saussure had not explored in detail how the meaning contained in the signified is organized, supposing that the sign-units composed of signifier–signified would stand in a relationship of contrast within the language system and that this differential relation would be sufficient to generate the meaning of each sign, and thus also to give content to each signified. Hjelmslev argued that the differential principle that defines the sign in Saussure's theory should be carried further into an analysis of how meaning is generated in language. In order to do so, one would have to establish a parallel between the construction of sound and the construction of meaning.

In the case of sound, a language defines within a sound continuum certain sounds as meaning-bearers, the so-called 'phonemes'. The phonemes are the differences in sound that are sufficient within that language to distinguish between words and thus to make a difference on the level of meaning. In order to describe how a language creates a system of phonemes out of the sound continuum, Hjelmslev uses the image of a net casting a shadow on a surface. The net itself consists of formal phonemic distinctions, pure sound traits. The shadows cast by the net when it is held up above the sound continuum demarcate sounds that will be phonemically significant in the language, the actual phonemes. Whereas the 'net' is a scientific reconstruction, the system of phonemes traced by the net in this model corresponds to the actual sound system of a particular language, i.e. its complete set of vowels and consonants.

If the image of the net and its shadow is applied to *meaning*, one gets a more nuanced concept of meaning than that of the 'signified' that equals a unit of content within the sign. In applying the model of the net, one can say that word meanings are generated when a net of formal distinctions is held up above a 'meaning continuum' on which it casts a shadow.

The 'net' of formal distinctions is defined by Hjelmslev as a 'form of content'. The net of phonemic distinctions on the level of sound is a 'form of expression'. The model thus has six terms: form of expression, sound continuum, phoneme, form of content, meaning continuum and meaning. This six-term model differs from Saussure's dual concept of the sign in semantic terms: for it is now not the coordination of meaning and sound *within the sign* that constitutes the basic building block of language. Sound and meaning are only coordinated once sound and meaning have been separately generated as phonemes and meanings within the language. Hjelmslev thus liberates the organization of meaning from its confinement within the sign, displaying a level of organization that is radically internal to language.

Deleuze and Guattari use Hjelmslev's concepts in isolation from their context within the science of linguistics. For the problem of semiotics that is explored in the Kafka book concerns a level of organization of signification that is prior to the order of signification that we find in language. This prior level of organization is, like the genetic order of sense in *The Logic of Sense*, a structuring or ordering process. It is, however, not an ordering of *sayables* and *thinkables*, but an ordering of the relationships that the human being can have to the world. These relationships are sexual, political, linguistic and, in a general sense, semiotic.

These different relationships are subordinated to a structuring dynamic which we can call a 'logic of desire'. A logic of desire is different from a logic of sense in that it takes place on the level of affect and sexual energy, considered as a field within which a human being is connected with its environment. Desire is organized into a 'logic' because different kinds of relationship are coordinated with one another in an ordered way.

The Hjelmslevian terms of form of expression and form of content are now employed to designate two poles within this logic of desire, two different kinds of relationship that desire establishes with its environment. The form of content is the spatial and affective relation between a body and its surroundings. The form of expression is a mode of representation – text or image – that this organization of the body is correlated with at a particular moment.

Just as in Hjelmslev's linguistic theory there is no direct *relationship of signification* between form of expression and form and content – since the form of expression relates to the sound continuum and the form of content to the meaning continuum, and the 'net' does not relate directly to the 'net', so to speak – equally for Deleuze and Guattari the coordination of form of expression and form of content is not a relationship of signification. The two are simply coordinated. This coordination constitutes an a-signifying logic of desire.

This logic of coordination is structurally analogous to the structure of parallelism in Spinoza's metaphysics. The divine substance expresses itself within the parallel modes of extension and thought. The relationship between the two attributes is not causal, thus for Spinoza an idea or mental representation cannot be the cause of a physical action. In the Kafka book, the logic of desire coordinates parallel forms of organization, of body (form of content) and 'mind' (form of expression) and there is no relationship of signification between the two. The problems that 'parallelism' and the logic of desire are meant to solve are not exactly the same in each case: Spinoza criticizes a common-sense view of the mind as having willpower over the body. Deleuze and Guattari seek to develop a materialist semiotics, in which desire, in its dual logic of expression, creates signification without, itself being the object of signification and representation. Nevertheless the analogy is instructive: parallelism is a strategy that serves to break the pragmatic connections of cause and meaning that we establish within experience.

Following this materialist semiotic premise, Deleuze and Guattari read Kafka's texts in such a way that they are not seen to signify or to symbolize an underlying problem of desire. Rather, they are seen to enact a movement of desire, expressed as a particular semiotic ordering process, coordinating in the texts, movements of the body and types of signification. This materialist semiotic strategy of reading raises the question of how to counter the apparently obvious symbolic, theological or psychoanalytic interpretations of his texts. Kafka's texts are often interpreted as symbolizing fear and guilt: fear of his own father and fear of marriage, fear of the bureaucracy and of the state. They are seen to be full of oppressive situations that could be interpreted as expressions of guilt.

With their materialist logic of desire, Deleuze and Guattari seek to overturn these symbolic interpretations. However, since their own semiotics of desire is very close to psychoanalysis, they have to define clearly how they differ from a psychoanalytic interpretation of Kafka's life and work starting from the premise that Kafka's life and work display an 'Oedipal' rivalry with his father, and a consequent problem of entering a stable heterosexual relationship. Given Kafka's fear of his father, described at length in the unpublished 'Letter to my father', and his protracted and well-documented anxiety concerning marriage – he had a long but finally interrupted engagement to Felice Bauer – there seems to be overwhelming biographical support for an Oedipal interpretation of either his life, his work or both. Now, Deleuze and Guattari do not deny this. They do not claim that Kafka's life does not display an Oedipal conflict, but they question the conceptual and explanatory role this conflict should have in our readings of his life and work. They question the commonly held belief that his texts are symbolic of this Oedipal conflict. Instead they shift the focus away from the text–life relationship towards an inverse life–text relationship and ask the very different question: what did Kafka have to do to transform this Oedipal conflict into a condition of writing? Deleuze and Guattari believe this problem of creation to be repeated within Kafka's texts themselves through the logic of desire that they construct.

In Kafka's stories, Deleuze and Guattari discover a treatment of Oedipal desire within a semiotic machine. The machine is constituted by a particular logic of desire, that is a particular coordination of form of content and form of expression. The form of content is a bowed head; the form of expression is a portrait: in the story *Metamorphosis*, the protagonist, Gregor Samsa who has become transformed into a beetle, at one moment glues himself with a bowed head to a portrait of a woman on the wall. The form of content (bowed head) and the form of expression (portrait) are joined by this connecting movement.

In so far as desire circulates within this coordination between form of content and form of expression, it constitutes a 'desiring machine'. The internal form of this particular desiring machine, the common formal element coordinating form of content and form of expression, is then at the same time a material factor influencing the way that desire circulates in the machine. In this case this material and formal element is that of a *block* or an *inhibition*. Both in its physical enactment (form of content) and in its entry into the semiotic realm (form of expression) desire is blocked and inhibited: the head is bent, the desired woman is obtained only as a portrait, as a representation. The machine thus configures a doubly blocked desire. It is blocked not with reference to an external impossibility – recognition by the father, marriage, and so on. It is blocked internally, within its own immanent movement. It is blocked once as bowed head and a second time as 'imaginarization', as the movement of desire towards an imaginary object 'portrait' rather than towards a concrete object, another person.

Desire in itself is here both a connecting synthesis (*Anti-Oedipus*) and a line of flight (*A Thousand Plateaus*). A blocked desire is thus a connection that is being made and a flight that does not take place. This movement of desire characterizes not only what happens *in* the stories but describes also the process of writing in Kafka's life. Through the concept of the desiring machine, Deleuze and Guattari establish a semiotic principle with which to analyse the life–writing relationship simultaneously from the point of view of life and from the point of view of writing – and to do so non-reductively and non-causally. Life and text are parallel enactments of the same machine.

The key problem of Kafka's life and writing process, as well as of his stories, is thus how desire finds a way out, how it avoids being blocked or turning sterile. This is precisely Kafka's problem as a writer within an Oedipal constellation: how to transform his menacing merchant-father into a condition of writing. This movement of creative appropriation–transformation covers, as well, Kafka's cultural and linguistic situation. He has to find a way of making his marginalized position as a German-speaking Jew in Prague into an aesthetic vantage point.

In the texts, this movement of escape is spatial. The dominant vector in Kafka's space is *contiguity*. The adjacent space juxtaposes events in an order of contiguity opposed to the symbolic order of ascendance towards a unitary principle such as God, the Father, or the State. Another type of movement is one of transformation, as in the stories of human beings becoming animals. These transformations have the character of a gradual movement of becoming (*devenir*). In both cases, in contiguous physical movement and in the continuous movement of becoming, the movement is immanent, it is internal to its coordinates, it needs no real or symbolic end point outside the movement.

Becoming animal absorbs and intensifies a previously given relation to a social environment. Kafka's struggle to conquer the space of writing is similarly a process of becoming in which, instead of confronting his aim or his obstacle directly, he gradually transforms a situation of impediment into a state of creativity. In the face of the father and the prospect of marriage he writes love letters to keep the beloved at a distance, then he passes through the form of the short story which is still a form of closure, until with the unfinished novels he accesses a stream of writing that is not closed by any external limit. Passing through the space of writing, Kafka changes his relation to guilt and to his family. Immanence is thereby conquered as a field that differentiates itself from its surroundings by a simultaneous movement of withdrawal and absorption.

This movement is also immanent in a different, semiotic sense. It constitutes an immanent trajectory of desire. What desire passes through along this trajectory is constituted by and within this movement as *intensive*, i.e. non-signifying, non-symbolic states. The intensities that desire passes through on its way do not refer to anything outside of themselves. The sense produced within the texts itself consists of intensive states. What we do as readers is equally to pass through these intensive states. The immanent process thereby absorbs all aspects of the work: language, life, society, textual events and images are parts of one movement of desire – and this movement has no outside. All questions which arise from Kafka's texts, whether ethical or political, are to be situated within this movement. The success criterion of the creative process as line of flight is whether it avoids an absolute withdrawal into self-destruction or a sterile withdrawal into an imaginary realm. Kafka's letters to Felice constitute such a dead end of desire. When, on the other hand, desire is unblocked as a movement of writing, a passage through language, language itself becomes a bearer of intensities rather than a means of representation. With this opposition between language as intensity and language as representation, Deleuze and Guattari formulate a further, aesthetic and political, distinction between classical and so-called 'minor' literature.

To be a classical writer one has to have access to a central viewpoint from which to represent the moral, cultural and political structures of a society. Minor literature, by contrast, views society from an oblique, marginal angle. It grasps the logic and the functioning of society rather than its dominant categories and self-images. With his drama *Faust*, Goethe created a representation of middle-class values and dilemmas (morality and sex, thought and action) in which subsequent generations of middle-class citizens could recognize themselves. That made Goethe a classical author. Joseph's Conrad's *Heart of Darkness*, by contrast, depicts English colonialism as a hell of barbarism and cruelty – and he can do so because he produces specific intensive states within the English language, liberating it from its conventional rhetorical virtues of wit, elegance and satire:

> They were dying slowly – it was very clear. They were not enemies, they were not criminals, they were nothing earthly now, – nothing but black shadows of disease and starvation, lying confusedly in the greenish gloom. Brought from all the recesses of the coast in all the legality of time contracts, lost in uncongenial surroundings, fed on unfamiliar food, they sickened, became inefficient, and were then allowed to crawl away and rest. These moribund shapes were free as air – and nearly as thin.[5]

The criteria for minority are twofold: language has to acquire a non-classical intensity and the world has to be appropriated as an immanent logic of desire rather than be represented according to its own moral categories. The criterion for minority is thus not membership in a minority. For a regional writer who ascribes a group identity to himself nearly always risks becoming imprisoned in a communal representation of himself and of his people – and for Deleuze and Guattari collective identifications of this kind are a way of blocking desire, not a means of creation.

Minor literature thus does not represent society but re-enacts its logic of desire, thereby connecting the order of the unconscious and

the structures of power in a given political context. This requires
that the writer establishes a direct and non-representational relation
to the desires circulating with the social realm. In order for language thus to become a vehicle of desire, in order for it to enter into
a direct relation with the social body, the representational level of
language has to be broken down. Through this breakdown of representation minor literature acquires a direct, or visionary relation
to social reality. The criterion of minority is thus not biographical
but ontological: minority literature is the re-enactment of a social
logic of desire, of what they call the *social machine*.

Kafka and the Social Machine

The movement of desire is by its very nature political, for desire in
Kafka's texts circulates through the social body, through the corridors of power, through the legal system. Power itself is thereby
eroticized. A striking feature of Kafka's novels is that meetings with
officials and with any other character often occur in places, such as
corridors and cellars, which are not the central or official places of
political activity. Often these places and meetings have a strong
erotic charge embodied in the women of the court and of the castle.
These women love indiscriminately the judges, the assistants and
the accused. Their desire is part of the political or legal institution.
Power thereby becomes directly involved in an erotic process which
has little in common with the representative function of judges and
officials.

Deleuze and Guattari thus take very seriously the expression, 'in
the corridors of power'. What happens in these corridors is the life
of power. This life is desire. Erotic desire is just one element of
the desire that is enacted as power. This desire-as-power functions
primarily as a movement of *connection*. The novels pursue this
movement as an essentially open-ended process, the movement
of a social desire which can by definition never have an end. The
movement of Joseph K is that of an individual desire entering the
social desire of the court. The social machine created by Kafka is a
desiring machine which knows no outside. There is nothing that
could be merely private or personal and which the social connection
machine would not be concerned with.

Now, to depict power in this way is not to *represent* society but to
absorb and then *speed up* the movement that already determines contemporary social reality. Kafka's novels exaggerate elements of social
reality and combine them into a new whole in which the social,

sexual and spatial configurations of power are displayed and brought out of control. Instead of criticizing society, Kafka's novels are thus machines which derail or *deterritorialize* the desire that circulates in the social machine. This movement of deterritorialization works through a semiotic principle of ordering that is called *serialization*. The principle of serialization had already been applied to the phenomenological concept of language and meaning in *The Logic of Sense*. It is now used to mount an attack on the concept of a self-identical individual subject: the notion of a subject that is only real if it is embodied and it is only embodied if it exists as one, self-identical, permanent individual. In the order of narrative this corresponds to the construction of stable characters who stand at the centre of the story, as both agents in the story and points of view on the world of the text. Oedipalization similarly requires a certain stability of individual identities and relationships: the father, the mother and the child have, at least in the child's mind, to occupy relatively stable positions. Serialization works against both of these principles of narrative identity and the structural stability of Oedipal positions. Kafka's novels *The Castle* and *The Trial* have fixed central characters, K and Joseph K, but these characters are surrounded by others who in their seriality refuse to enter fixed and stable relationships.

These series tend to extend and to multiply. The court will have an ever extending series of judges, the castle has an unlimited series of officials and each element within a series can multiply by opening up a new sub-series of connections. Second, the serialization of characters disrupts the closure entailed by duality and triangular relations. Dual and triangular relations are stable in the short stories where the family is not inscribed within a larger political machine. In the novels, the dual and the triangular relations are opened up by the serial relations of the social machine in which any character becomes inscribed. Third, the eroticization of the political machine is itself serial. The young women who make love to the hero and help him in his dealings with the authorities are part sisters, part whores but they never occupy an Oedipal relation of parent or spouse. They function as *connectors*, as points of communication in the machines of the court and the castle.

This systematic serialization of social and sexual relations pushes desire in the direction of ever further deterritorialization, making desire more and more desire, operating increasingly on a plane of connectivity and contiguity unbound by place and social function. This open-ended connectivity slowly undermines the individual identity of the central character-subject, detaching it from any

specific function or social position. Yet these characters are neither able to affirm or endorse this gradual slipping away of their selfhood. For, as Deleuze and Guattari wrote in *Anti-Oedipus* and will continue to write in *A Thousand Plateaus*, desire is in essence *ambivalence*, torn between a movement of ever greater uprooting or deterritorialization and a reaffirmation of social identity against this movement of destabilization. This contrary movement, which they call paranoid-fascist in *Anti-Oedipus*, is also present in Kafka's enactments of desire.

Characters are not only serialized, they are also *segmented*, that is, positioned and classified as socially well-defined individuals. They occupy their positions and their territories, affirming their particular functions within the social machine. The main character will often be exempt from this segmentation as he comes into contact with the social or legal machine at different points of its functioning – K. is a surveyor without a clear assignment and Joseph K is a citizen seeking knowledge about 'his' legal case. These characters at the same time nurture a craving for certainty and social recognition, for a fixed identity in relation to the social machine; in short, they seek to reterritorialize themselves within the social machine.

The same ambiguity, between a dissolving, deterritorializing movement of desire and its contrary reterritorializing impulse, exists within the social machine itself as a conflict between hierarchical and socially well-defined relations, on the one hand, and relations that are not as defined, spatial relations of connectivity and contiguity, on the other. This ambivalence in the social machine is not simply invented by Kafka but corresponds to a historical and political reality. It expresses a condition of modern bureaucracy, caught between an ancient hierarchical institution model of and a modern mode of functioning based on the circulation of people, information and capital.

We have thus arrived at a point where the critique of representation in its psychoanalytic and semiotic forms – the Oedipal schema of interpretation, the Saussurean dualist idealism – have given place to the description of Kafka's semiotic machine as it re-enacts a social logic of power and desire. Re-enactment, connectivity, serialization are the formal textual operations which articulate desire between the poles of Oedipal and social definition, on the one hand, and open-ended connection-repetition, on the other. This is not a representation of desire since desire is not mapped according to thematic – moral-social – divisions.

3

A History of the Modern Subject

Semiotics, Servitude, Subjectivity

Anti-Oedipus presents an elaborate theory of political power and the relationship between the individual and society. This theory situates the political question of obedience within an ontological account of social reality. In this theory of social reality power and obedience are analysed from a very different perspective from the one adopted in classical political theory seeking to classify types of government often with the aim of identifying the best, most just form of government and use of state of power.

In *Anti-Oedipus*, power is not analysed as the property of the state and its representatives. State power is instead analysed in terms of how it functions. In *Anti-Oedipus*, power is a cognitive and semiotic system. Power manifests itself as a cognitive and signifying system through which a society is held together. This is why the theory of power refers to a general ontology of society. According to this ontology, societies always produce systems of self-representation through which they 'inscribe' authority onto a semiotic surface of sense. This process is engendered by and within an immense process, a circulation of energy that encompasses every member of social reality, all power, wealth and land. This energy process is the basis of social reality, its material substance.

The semiotic surface of inscription is the self-representation that this process produces of itself. Power becomes authority, that is, becomes effective and binding on individuals only through this semiotic process of inscription. Thus, the basic categories of society are not free-standing individuals and instances of power and authority, but poles of energy relating to each other in terms of categories inscribed on the semiotic surface of sense.

The aim of this elaborate social ontology is ethical rather than political. Concerned neither with justice nor with social change, the theory of power that they present on the basis of this social ontology is aimed at analysing the cognitive and semiotic effects of certain types of power and authority upon the individual subject and to show how and if it would be possible for us, living now, in Western capitalist societies to relate differently, through different cognitive and semiotic systems, to these forms of power and authority.

As Eugene Holland has shown,[1] *Anti-Oedipus* stands in a rich twentieth-century philosophical tradition of thinkers who, combining psychoanalysis and Marxism, have sought to analyse the modern individual as a site of oppressions that are in part self-inflicted. Deleuze and Guattari differ from other writers in this tradition, such as Marcuse, in their highly theoretical and epistemological approach to both psychoanalysis and Marxism. They are thus not seeking to combine a psychoanalytic theory of the mind with a Marxist social theory in order to arrive at an all-encompassing general theory of the economy and the unconscious. Instead they produce a critique of psychoanalysis that serves as a means to formulate their own theory of subjectivity. This theory of subjectivity is elaborated within a larger critical, historical and semiotic framework.

The elaboration of this framework is inspired mainly by Kant, Marx and Nietzsche. What Deleuze and Guattari take from these three thinkers is a perspective on the individual human subject as being something *produced* and *created*. This derivative status of the individual subject is different from the dependence of the conscious on unconscious drives in psychoanalysis. Both Freud and Lacan, who are the two psychoanalytic theorists at the centre of the discussion here, assume a certain individualistic perspective within their methodologies. This psychoanalytic individualism consists in assuming that the individuals who are the objects of analysis and cure also define the horizon of explanation within the cure. Thus, neither social structure, historical conditions nor other layers of reality that encompass the individual subject are allowed to dominate the psychoanalytic explanation.

Deleuze and Guattari now advance the general charge against psychoanalysis that their epistemological individualism has made them the perfect spokesmen of capitalist societies and of the organization of power within these societies. This attack is tempered by the acknowledgement that psychoanalysis by becoming this voice and symptom of the contemporary world also functions as a perfect way of entry into the politics and ethics of oppression within capitalist societies.

In other words, psychoanalysis is a privileged object of study for political theory because of its sophisticated negation of all the conditions that shape the individual subject beyond the structure of its own psyche, but the privilege of psychoanalysis stretches further than this. In fact, Freud and Lacan have with their theory of the Oedipus complex correctly identified the nature of subjectivity under capitalism.

What they have not correctly understood, however, and what the social ontology and historical and semiotic analysis of *Anti-Oedipus* will set right, is that this form of subjectivity is itself a *surface phenomenon*, the outcome of a complex historical-semiotic process. The subject is the effect of a process and hence the concept of the subject cannot serve as an ultimate explanatory principle or form the horizon of an analysis of itself!

The argument of *Anti-Oedipus* is thus rather complex in that it involves at least the following three strands:

1 a semiotic and ontological theory of *power*;
2 a genealogical account of modern *subjectivity*;
3 an epistemological critique of *psychoanalysis*.

Thus, (1) the semiotic and ontological theory of power forms the basis for (2) a genealogical account of modern subjectivity developed through the prism of (3) an epistemological critique of psychoanalysis.

As this summary makes clear, the ethical and political dimensions of *Anti-Oedipus* are embedded in arguments that are either ontological, semiotic or epistemological. The focal point of these arguments is the concept of the subject. The following discussion presents the general argumentative structure of the book while devoting particular attention to the genealogy of the subject and the semiotic theory of power on which it is grounded.

Political Theory

The originality of *Anti-Oedipus*, within political theory, lies in articulating the relationship between state and citizen on the unconscious level of sexual energy and analysing the encounter between this energy and the state as a relation that is only possible if society produces a surface of inscription or sense on which it can define its own categories of authority, thereby signifying and representing to the members of society the form and meaning of obedience.

This is the theoretical framework of *Anti-Oedipus*, but the precise political question concerning obedience, that is the question of why members of a society obey the laws and the state, can itself be formulated in two opposing ways. It can either be formulated as a question of justification: why is it rational for citizens to obey the state? Why is it in their best interest to do so? This is the Hobbesian version of the question, the version that continues in the 'social contract' tradition that culminates with Hegel. This tradition understands the social realm and political power as being in need of a justification and it appeals to the notion of individual rational self-interest as the ground for this justification. If one can show that it is better for the individual to obey the state than not to, one has presented a *case for authority*, one has presented the force of political rule as a common good. This is not the version of the question that is endorsed by Deleuze and Guattari.

Their question is not why it is good to obey, but, given that obedience, docility, and social conformism cannot be part of our nature as bearers of free or unbound and directionless sexual energy, how then could we have become the adapted, law-abiding subjects that we undoubtedly are? This is a Nietzschean version of the problem of obedience. Nietzsche thought that the development of morality was a development against our nature, or against our instincts, and that the emergence of morality in human history thus required an explanation that would account for this departure from our nature.

The question of obedience is further given a particular historical angle by Deleuze and Guattari. The past two hundred years of capitalism have produced a growth of parliamentary democracy and individual freedoms, as well as an erosion of traditional forms of authority. How then can it be that the modern individual or subject under capitalism is so law-abiding, apparently so happy to conform to the requirements of the society and of the market? Their answer to this question, put simply, is: because the modern subject is one that has learnt to say no to its desire. The modern subject is autonomous, outwardly, but in relation to itself and especially in relation to its own desire, it has learnt to exercise severe control.

This modern subject is exactly like the sexual subject theorized by psychoanalysis as having gone through the Oedipal complex:

desiring his mother, the boy learns that the position of lover in relation to this desired object is already occupied, namely by his own
father. The boy therefore hates his father as a rival. The boy must
learn to overcome this aggression. He can do so if he can realize
that he may transfer his desire from the mother to other women,
and thus that he too can occupy the structural position of the father,
i.e. the position as lover and as father, but in relation to another
woman. The transformation of aggression into identification also
implies that the boy accepts the father's sanctioning of his own
desire for the mother, thereby to some extent taking over this sanctioning authority and exercising it towards himself. For Deleuze
and Guattari, the Oedipus theory and the subject it describes are
exemplary of the condition of subjectivity under capitalism.

A further set of questions, however, remain: why would capitalism produce the Oedipal subject, and how? In response to these
questions, *Anti-Oedipus* develops an argument with many different
strands and components. If we focus on the question of how the
Oedipal subject is produced, we can perhaps divide this part of the
argument of *Anti-Oedipus* into two separate accounts. One concerns
the nature of the *psyche*, the difference between desire in its natural
state and desire once it has become channelled through the Oedipus
complex. A second account concerns the political implications of the
Oedipal subject within capitalism.

The general argument concerning modern subjectivity is the following: *a subject is produced through 'Oedipalization' of sexual energy.*
This Oedipal transformation takes place within the family and is
conditioned by the family. The Oedipal process is a change from an
immanent to a representational channelling of sexual energy, a
move from desire existing as a circuit of energy to a representational system of desire in which it is correlated with a determinate
and differentiated social space. Within this representational space
the subject is able to identify different individuals with a determinate social identity, i.e. father, mother and itself. This process of
transformation also entails the production of a subject within the
psyche who identifies itself as a social individual.

This new subject occupies an ambiguous position in relation to
its own sexual desire: within the psyche it occupies the position of
a law-giver, but at the same time it is able to transgress, at least on
an imaginary level, the law that it has given to itself: i.e. it defines
as incest, hence as forbidden and transgressive, the sexual act with
the mother, but since this act does not take place, the incest is *only*
imaginary. Yet as the subject comes into being precisely through the

rivalry over the mother as object of desire, it has to position itself in relation to this imaginary incest. Thus, the Oedipal subject is a subject who lives in constant fear of its own imaginary crime. Therefore it is also a subject who is eager to keep itself in check, to censor and to control itself.

This inclination towards self-control in turn fills a social and political vacuum. For the capitalist state is weak, and capitalism has eroded the conventional forms of authority that would create order in a pre-capitalistic society. Capitalism erodes state authority because it replaces one signifying system with another. It replaces a system of codification and representation of the social realm with a purely formal system of equivalences which is not representational.

A pre-capitalist state produces a system of representation through which it can codify and represent all practices and all desires within its domain. Therefore the authority of the pre-capitalist state is embodied in this system of representation. For only within a system of representation is it possible to codify desire. Capitalism, however, relies on a principle of formal equivalence, equivalence between price and merchandise, between the value of the merchandise and the labour time consumed in producing it, and so on. These relationships of formal equivalence are not representational or signifying, they are abstractly formal. Capitalism erodes authority because it uproots or deterritorializes the representational sign system of the pre-capitalist state.

The state under capitalism is weakened by this deterritorialization. It is threatened by a collective mass of sexual desire that has not been codified, for desire is, in the political theory of *Anti-Oedipus*, the primary object of control and the object on which political power as codification is first of all exercised. The reterritorializing capitalist state thus gives itself the task of codifying desire. Since, however, it is not itself equipped with a codifying machine, the task of codifying desire is transferred to the family and further to the individual who constructs the Oedipal subject as a mechanism of codification.

In the rest of this chapter I will try to elucidate this political and semiotic critique of the subject, by separating further the different components of the account.

Critique

The social and psychological theory of *Anti-Oedipus* is formulated through a critique of Freudian and Lacanian psychoanalysis. The notion of 'critique' as I use it here refers to the way the term is defined, on the one hand, by Kant and, on the other, by Marx. In both these authors, 'critique' does not consist in arguing directly against an adversary, but is a much more complex and indirect procedure. Critique is a form of analysis that examines a certain, usually conventional and common sense, mode of thought in order to lay bare its underlying assumptions. These assumptions are *conditions* of that mode of thought, but nevertheless, they are not, indeed cannot, be made explicit within that thought itself. Critique thus implies an element of revelation. A mode of thought is criticized when assumptions that it was unaware of but which are its necessary conditions are brought to light.

This critique of common-sense thinking as based on unconscious assumptions and conditions thus also implies a complete change of perspective in relation to the perspective of common sense which is usually non-reflective, spontaneous, non-theoretical.

Critique in this sense is the precursor of the twentieth-century 'critical theory' of Adorno and Horkheimer and of French post-structuralism in so far as these intellectual movements aim at replacing a common-sense, and in both cases, individualistic view on the world with a more complex theoretical account of reality in which the individualistic perspective has its own, limited, place. For Deleuze, the common-sense point of view is identified as the representational perspective on reality. In *Anti-Oedipus*, he and Guattari seek to produce a materialist critique of the representationalist perspective and its cognitive models, as these methods are exemplified by psychoanalysis, and more precisely by the theoretical description of cognitive processes within psychoanalysis.

The critical method employed in *Anti-Oedipus* to uncover the underlying assumptions of this psychoanalytic theory of the psyche combines elements of Kant's *transcendental critique* of reason and Marx's *materialist critique* of so-called 'classical political economy', i.e. the liberal economic theory of Adam Smith and David Ricardo.

Kant's transcendental method seeks to uncover the universal logical and cognitive presuppositions of all empirical, and especially scientific, judgements about the world. These presuppositions cannot be validated by those empirical scientific judgements themselves. Only a separate account, a transcendental critique, can show how the empirical use of reason operates. Marx's critique is historical and materialistic. It examines the central concepts of classical economic theory – money, value, labour – and argues that these terms derive their meaning from a historical and economic structure of production which classical economic theory is unable to account for. The critical method adopted in *Anti-Oedipus* has traits in common with both Kant's transcendental analysis and Marx's historical materialism.

Psychoanalytic theory, as developed mainly by Freud and Lacan, is examined in great detail in *Anti-Oedipus* so as to make explicit its underlying organizing principles. Some of the basic principles of psychoanalysis are endorsed by Deleuze and Guattari:

1   The psyche consists of sexual energy that it processes without the intervention of conscious thought.
2   Sexual desire is the object of repression within the psyche and this repression originates in an internalized instance of authority.

These principles are both, according to *Anti-Oedipus*, true, but their truth is not fully known or explained by psychoanalysis itself. For instance, psychoanalysis fails to consider the historical conditions of psychic censorship or repression. The English word 'repression' is ambivalent in this context. On the one hand, it translates the French word 'refoulement', itself a translation of the German 'Verdrängung', referring to the operation of censorship within the psyche. On the other hand, 'repression' can refer to the social pressures exercised against desire and sexuality within the bourgeois family. Deleuze and Guattari produce a critique of 'repression' in both these senses of the word. It concerns precisely the relationship between these two kinds of repression – the relationship, in other words, between psychic censorship and the social control of sexuality.

The claim that psychoanalysis is unable to conceptualize the political dimension of this social repression of desire constitutes the Marxian dimension of their critique. They also argue that psychoanalysis is incapable of adequately analysing the internal logical and cognitive relations produced by and within the unconscious. This is the Kantian dimension of their project.

Kant not only sought to establish the domain about which we may legitimately produce judgements, that is, the domain over which our logical categories may range without producing unverifiable statements; he also sought to analyse the contradictions we produce when we apply these categories outside of the empirical realm. One area in which it is almost inevitable that we overstretch our cognitive faculties is the area that we ourselves are, namely our inner life. For Kant thinks it is very difficult for us to realize that the inner life is an empirical reality and thus subject to a law of dispersion: what is empirical can never appear except as spread out either in space and time (outer sense) or in time only (inner sense). Therefore, we want to attribute to the succession of mental states that make up our inner life, a *substantial unity*. This would not be a material unity, the unity of a body, but the unity of a spiritual thing or soul. This spiritual thing is then easily assumed to possess the properties ascribed to the soul by Christian theology, the properties of indivisibility, immateriality, permanence, and so on. However, the assumption that our inner life possesses this kind of substantiality and the subsequent attribution of metaphysical properties to this substance are operations of a completely different nature from the simplicity and unity they seek to articulate. Just as empirical experience for Kant is constructed out of a combination of categories applied to a sensory manifold, so the application of these categories outside of the sensory realm also involves a series of separate steps. By analysing these successive steps, Kant presents a genetic account of the operations that produce the idea of a substantial self:

> From these elements [the categories], at least through composition, spring all the concepts of the pure doctrine of the soul, without any other principle being cognized in the least. This substance, merely as an object of inner sense, gives us the concept of *immateriality*; as simple substance, it gives us that of *incorruptibility*; its identity, as an intellectual substance, gives us the *personality*; all these points together [alle diese drei Stücke zusammen] *spirituality*.[2]

In thus producing the Idea of a substantial Self or Soul the mind transcends what is empirically given in inner and outer sense; it makes a transcendent use of the categories. Kant calls this transcendent use of the categories a 'paralogism'.

Deleuze and Guattari argue that the construction of an Oedipal subject within the psyche entails a similar constructive process, passing through a series of discrete steps which in their composition produce a new entity, which is a socially defined subject of desire correlated with a whole person, or discernible individual, as object of desire. As in Kant, this process involves the use of cognitive operations – the syntheses through which sexual energy is processed in the psyche. As in Kant, these syntheses must in order to produce the Oedipal subject be led away from their normal functioning within their own domain (the circuit of sexual energy in the psyche) in order to be assigned a transcendent use (correlation with discernible individuals). They call this use of the syntheses of the psyche its 'paralogisms'.

This appropriation of Kant constitutes a first step in a genetic critique of the subject, an analysis that seeks to show that the Oedipal subject is not a *natural given* but the product of a genetic process. The next step in this critique is a history of signifying systems seen as a condition for the cognitive and semiotic structure of the Oedipus subject. This step in their critique is established through an appropriation of Marx's critique of the individualist principles of classical political economy and of so-called German Ideology, the term Marx uses to designate contemporary social philosophers such as Feuerbach and Stirner.

In Marx's theory of society, economic activity, social relations and political systems are conceived as belonging to one overarching, and historically specific, socio-economic structure. Within this structure, what one could think of as separate activities or levels of reality are in fact never separate but only become intelligible in their historical meaning according to their place and role within the total socio-economic structure. It is the main point of Marx's critique of so-called classical political economists such as Adam Smith that they failed to see this structural interdependence between different layers of society and the economy and thus treated economic activity separately from the configuration of social relations, i.e. the division of labour and relations of property, on which economic activity is founded according to Marx's conception of the socio-economic structure.

Marx's social philosophy is based on the premise that all human activity is *intelligible*. No thing is ever beyond the reach of understanding, but also no thing is ever intelligible in isolation, as it appears immediately to an individual. For Marx, immediacy is the relation to the world of an *abstract individual*, i.e. an individual that has not become intelligible against the background of historical conditions that define that individual. The socio-economic embodiment of this abstract individual under capitalism is the private property holder.

Now the primary target of Marx's critique of classical economy and liberal political philosophy is the notion that this private property holder should be considered the origin and universal condition for economic activity. Thereby what is an *effect* is taken to be a *cause* and a particular historical condition, bourgeois industrial society, is taken to be a universal economic condition. Marx does not deny that individual economic agents play an important role within a capitalist economy, but his critique consists in asking what the existence of such individual agents presupposes on the level of social organization.

In parallel to this critique of classical political economy, Marx attacks German social philosophers such as Stirner and Feuerbach who had sought to analyse social relations from the point of view of autonomous individuals and in particular from the perspective of these individuals' subjective and self-conscious positioning of themselves in relation to society. Thereby, they too reverse the order of explanation and treat as a natural given and a first principle what is in fact an effect, a historical product. For in Marx's view, even ideas and mental activity are real and part of human history in so far as they are a function of economic activity and of the social relations surrounding economic activity: 'The production of ideas, of conceptions, of consciousness, is at first directly interwoven with the material activity and the material intercourse of men, the language of real life. Conceiving, thinking, the mental intercourse of men, appear at this stage as the direct efflux of their material behaviour.'[3] This materialist conception is not adopted directly by Deleuze and Guattari, but the critical principle that ideas, mental activity and the inner life are historical products and not natural givens and that they therefore cannot figure as principles of explanation is taken over directly in *Anti-Oedipus*. It is thus the critical aim of *Anti-Oedipus* to show that nothing ever begins in an individual subject. No decision or agency which can be ascribed to an individual subject is ever intelligible simply as the decision or agency of that subject. This is a continuation of the critique of the subject undertaken in Deleuze's previous works. If there is a subject, this subject is a site of affects and processes and a result of other processes.

The structure of *Anti-Oedipus* is shaped by these critical tasks, to define the historical conditions of social and psychic repression and to uncover a transcendental logic of the unconscious, conceived as a cognitive apparatus. Deleuze and Guattari's critique of psychoanalysis, and of the Oedipal Subject which Freud theorizes, thus involves a series of steps.

First, they formulate a theory of the psyche as a cognitive apparatus. Second, they show how this cognitive apparatus, under the effect of social pressures enacted by the family, is transformed so that it produces the Oedipal Subject. Third, they analyse the historical and semiotic conditions of this Oedipal Subject through a theory of capitalism that is adapted from Marx. Fourth, they connect the transcendental and the materialist argument by asking the question: why does the Oedipal Subject emerge within capitalism? This fourth argument goes beyond the framework of critique sketched so far in that it does not just point to an underlying – cognitive, semiotic or social – structure or process, but involves establishing a link between completely separate types of argument and domains of reality. The inspiration for this fourth, and most ambitious, part of the argument in *Anti-Oedipus* is taken from Nietzsche.

In his *On the Genealogy of Morals*, Nietzsche undertakes a historical and cultural critique of moral psychology. The object of this critique is moral conscience. He asks the question: what does it mean to have moral conscience? But he does not ask this question in the abstract, he asks it in the context of a general theory of human beings, or anthropology. He thus asks, what does it mean for beings like us to have moral conscience? He assumes that we are beings driven by raw and spontaneous instincts, beings, therefore, for whom the kind of memory and reflexivity that conscience implies do not come naturally. The morality of guilt and responsibility is thus a movement against our own nature. But how then, Nietzsche continues, was it possible for us to develop conscience and morality if this was not in our nature? He argues that a long development within the entire history of humanity was necessary for this cultural and psychological structure to take root. He answers that humanity had to be *taught* memory. It had to learn to remember its own acts. This could only happen through the repeated experience of corporeal punishment and severe violence inflicted on the human body. The memory of each individual has thus been put in place through a process of learning that passed from generation to generation, forming a collective cultural educational process. Nietzsche calls this critical perspective *genealogical*.

A 'genealogy' is normally a map of one's ancestors. A genealogical critique looks at the ancestors of one's psychological instincts and moral beliefs within a collective cultural memory. This genealogical perspective entails the notion of a cultural memory that has a longer time span than that of individual societies or epochs. Genealogy is thus a trans-historical method. It does not just look at how something *evolves* through history but at how something is *sedimented* in cultural memory through the survival of past cultural forms within new social conditions. The trans-historical genealogical perspective is crucial for the overall structure of *Anti-Oedipus*. For it is only through such a genealogical framework that the transcendental and the materialist arguments can be fused into one.

The further implication of the genealogical perspective on morality is that moral conscience and self-reflection are not universal and ideal structures. They are the products of a specific, historical and material, process which transformed the animals that we are by making them turn their own vital instincts against themselves, thereby producing an 'inner life':

> Every instinct which does not vent itself externally *turns inwards* – this is what I call the *internalization* of man. It is at this point that what is later called the 'soul' first develops in man. The whole inner world, originally stretched thinly as between two membranes, has been extended and expanded, has acquired depth, breadth, and height in proportion as the external venting of human instinct has been *inhibited*.[4]

This intimate conceptual link between self-negation and interiority is a guiding idea also in *Anti-Oedipus*. Before entering into a more detailed exposition of the Oedipalization argument, it is necessary to turn to Freudian and Lacanian psychoanalysis which is the initial object of critique in *Anti-Oedipus*.

The Social and Logical Critique of Psychoanalysis

There are three different strands in Deleuze and Guattari's reading of psychoanalysis. First, there are elements in psychoanalysis which they take over and transform, such as the principle of the *unconscious* and the theory of *repression*: the unconscious processes sexual energy and internalizes mechanisms of censorship and control. Second, according to *Anti-Oedipus*, psychoanalysis correctly describes a structure of desire in the theory of the Oedipus complex. This Oedipal theory at the same time reflects a particular historical condition, namely the position of desire within society under capitalism. Psychoanalytic theory is not, due to its ahistorical and idealistic and hermeneutic method, capable of understanding its own place within history. Third, the psychoanalytic cure is to be replaced by a schizoanalytic treatment which will not aim to reintegrate the subject into society but will interact directly with the unconscious. It will seek to liberate libidinal energy from the socially adapted personality structure of the Oedipal 'system' of control in order for this energy to be released within social reality as a revolutionary force. We shall now look mainly at the second level of their reading, the way in which psychoanalysis adequately reflects a specific historical type of desire.

The socially defined individual with a definite personal identity, in other words, the concept of a *separate* and *identifiable* person, is analysed by Deleuze and Guattari as a category which is alien to the flow of sexual energy in the psyche but which can become imposed on the psyche through a specific process of transformation. The flow of desire in the psyche fixates itself only on particular sensations and physical encounters with other bodies. Neither these sensations nor these encounters are represented in the psyche as belonging within the organized structures of identifiable individual persons. For the psyche constitutes an immanent circuit of desire. The relations that it produces therefore do not correspond to the logical grid of identification and differentiation that the representation of the individual person requires.

In other words, the sensations that desire flows through are not logically ordered and the correlates of these sensations are what they call partial bodies rather than whole, socially identified persons. The name for immanence within this circuit of desire is the 'machine'. The machine is a relationship between desire, sensation and a part of the environment which can only be felt and thought from inside its coordinates and the energy that runs through them. This machine-desire corresponds exactly to what Freud calls the polymorphous perversity of infantile sexuality. Freud characterizes infantile sexuality as being either auto-erotic or directed towards others, and as being oriented towards body parts taken in isolation from the rest of the body rather than towards whole people. This polymorphous sexuality is epitomized in the act of sucking in which individual body parts are singled out for attention:

> A portion of the lip itself, the tongue, or any other part of the skin within reach – even the big toe – may be taken as the object upon which this sucking is carried out. In this connection a grasping-instinct may appear and may manifest itself as a simultaneous rhythmic tugging at the lobes as the ears or a catching hold of some part of another person (as a rule the ear) for the same purpose.[5]

For Freud, normal sexual development is one which leads away from this polymorphous desire and auto-erotic excitability, towards a goal directed, we could say, intentional structure of desire, aiming towards intercourse with a person of the opposite sex. Thus an infant desires indiscriminately, itself or parts of itself and parts of other objects, but normal development culminates in the constitution of a sexuality in which one person desires another person with the aim of intercourse. Desire is thereby defined by the alternative: either a relation to a whole individual (normal heterosexual behaviour) or a deviance from this norm (perversion).

There is in Freud's writings an ambiguity both with regard to relations of authority between individuals occupying a definite, either superior or inferior social position, and with regard to the moral perceptions of sexuality in the society in which he wrote. He is aware of relations of authority as it applies to his own case – he is sensitive to the issue of his own social position as a Jew for instance – but he is at the same time reluctant to perceive social structures of authority within the family and within society as a whole as contributing to the aetiology of a patient and thus as part of a psychoanalytic account. His views on morality are similarly ambivalent. As a scientist he seeks to bracket moral prejudices on sexual behaviour and he is well aware that his discoveries and theoretical claims may be socially and morally controversial. He thus sees sexuality as opposed to existing social norms, but, within the cure and the case studies, he never appears to challenge the moral authority of people occupying a social position of power. Apart from his own generally cautious and conservative mentality, he is prevented from challenging existing social structures and moral conventions for theoretical reasons, namely because of his deeply held belief that the psychoanalytic explanation has to be internal to the mental apparatus, i.e. to the productivity of the unconscious as it battles with repressed wishes. In psychoanalysis, this means that social authority is never allowed to become an explanatory factor, and that the repression of desire is always to be seen as a censorship carried out in and by the psyche, accomplished by an internal agency within the unconscious.

This principle is one of the main objects of criticism in *Anti-Oedipus*. If the unconscious is only understood from within the horizon of its own representations, it is seen only as a field where these representations occur and not as a process of production in which sexuality is directly involved with authority and power. *Anti-Oedipus* thus argues that the principle of explanatory autonomy of the unconscious leads to an idealism of the unconscious, obscuring the social reality of desire. They seek to overcome this idealism by analysing the psyche within a materialist, genetic and semiotic framework.

Anti-Oedipus also challenges Freudian analysis at an ontological level. Freud assumes that the category of the socially defined individual, the person possessing a definite identity within the family and within society, constitutes the natural correlate of desire. It is only if the subject, perversely, stays within infantile sexuality or goes through the Oedipal complex unsuccessfully, that desire remains attached to parts of the body or has other sexual aims than intercourse. This reproductive conception of sex treats as natural what is in fact the product of a social process of production, according to *Anti-Oedipus*. Freud identifies the reality of unconscious sexual energy, but confines this energy within a concept of a socially integrated individual. Deleuze and Guattari form the project of returning to the nature of desire as a reality that undermines the identity of these socially defined individuals.

At the same time as taking socially defined individuals as the end point of treatment, the starting point for explanation and the normal result of socio-sexual development, Freud accounts for the internal dynamics of the psyche in terms of energy and systems of competing agencies within the psyche. Freud thereby shows allegiance to two different scientific paradigms: the psyche is a system of energy but the psyche is also a cognitive system operating very much like conscious, rational agents. The principle of the unconscious does not solve the conflict but maintains it since the unconscious is conceived by Freud as a system existing within an individual. At the same time, the individual is represented within the system as an 'I' (Ich), seeking to assert control over the other forces and agencies in the system.

The psychoanalysis of Jacques Lacan solves some of the methodological tensions arising in Freud's theory from his concept of the socially defined individual. Lacan opposes the ontological category of the social individual to a purely structural concept of the subject of speech which is never identical with its embodiments in actual social individuals. The subject is also very different from Freud's concept of the rational 'I' as we will see.

Lacan defines the subject by distinguishing it from what he calls the *ego*. The ego is engendered by an imaginary and narcissistic relation to itself. The subject, by contrast, constitutes itself through language as a relation to others. It follows that the subject cannot be constituted within the inner space of feeling and introspection but has to be understood within a structure of intersubjectivity, situated within an Oedipal triangle. This Oedipal triangle is, however, not identical to the social and empirical structure of relations within the family. It is an ideal structure of representation in which the subject defines itself unconsciously in relation to a figure of paternal authority, the Name of the Father, in Lacan's terms. The subject itself is also not a person or an individual but a function and a position within this structure of representation.

To become a subject depends on entering a space of intersubjectivity which Lacan calls the symbolic order and which he identifies with language: when we enter the scene of language, we engage others in a relation of reciprocity. Or more precisely, when we use language, we relate to ourselves as beings defined by our relations to others. Apart from this reciprocal structure, the subject has no actual physical being or reality. To be a subject is to hold a certain position within language with regard to desire, as this desire is posited in relation to (the structural function of) paternal authority. As the subject is merely a position within the symbolic order the only agency we can refer to in the subject is the symbolic ordering process itself which Lacan calls the 'signifying chain'.

The formalism of this theory of the subject is evident in Lacan's re-interpretation of Freud's case history of Senatspräsident Schreber. This patient suffers from a delirium of persecution, involving the belief that the human race is doomed unless he, Schreber, is transformed by God into a woman. For Freud, this illness can be explained as resulting from a repressed homosexual desire originating in Schreber's relationship with his father. For Lacan, on the other hand, Schreber's state of being is determined by his incapacity to enter the symbolic order. He is not simply, as Freud says, *repressing* something (a homosexual desire), he is operating a much more fundamental denial. He *forecloses* (German: *verwerfen*) the transcendental condition of symbolization on which intersubjectivity, and thus subjectivity, depend. Lacan calls the *primary signifier* the transcendental function of language which demarcates this symbolic realm. It is this primary signifier which is foreclosed by Schreber. Foreclosing his entry into the symbolic order, Schreber excludes himself from common social reality and develops his own reality, his own system of beliefs, outside of the social world.

The discussion of Lacan in *Anti-Oedipus* is centred on the concepts of foreclosure and the symbolic order. Deleuze and Guattari approve of Lacan's formalization of the Oedipus complex because it introduces a distance to the social form of the reproductive individual which Freud treats as a natural given, but they argue that Lacan's formalization does not go far enough. It is still based on the triangular structure of the family – even if the members of that structure are reduced to functions. Lacan's concepts of foreclosure and the symbolic order also preserve the political implications of Freudian analysis – shared by medical psychiatry – namely, that mental illness is seen as a loss of reality, a withdrawal from a shared social world into a closed, private realm of delirium. The concept of foreclosure simply translates this common-sense and scientific opposition between madness and social reality into a formal model. For Lacan, we are all a little mad because we have to relate to what we cannot symbolize (the real), but as long as we have entered the symbolic order we are at least safely within social reality. The psychotic, on the other hand, has left this social reality behind and retreated into the world of his own imaginary inventions.

On the other hand, Lacan's formalization goes too far, according to Deleuze and Guattari, in denying the social and material reality of the unconscious. Desire for Lacan is ineffable; it equals a non-being whose only manifestation is its own distorted presence within the signifying chain. This idealism of desire and the signifying chain means that the Oedipal structure is socially non-specific. The authority that the subject has to confront in order to posit its desire within the symbolic order is never a concrete social authority, but the formal authority of the father as a function within the structure.

At this point there is a leap in the argument of *Anti-Oedipus*, a movement from a meta-critique of psychoanalysis to a transcendental, materialist and genealogical critique of its central ontological categories of the individual and the subject. It will turn out that Freud's individual and Lacan's subject correspond to two different aspects of the modern Oedipal subject as it is uncovered by this threefold critique. The critique of psychoanalysis is thus only a route towards a much deeper, ontological and historical problem of the genesis of the modern subject and the modern individual. We can now begin to retrace the steps of this more fundamental critique, starting with their own theory of the psyche.

From the Psyche to Oedipus

Deleuze and Guattari follow Freud in conceiving of the psyche as a cognitive system processing unconscious sexual energy. According to Freud, this energy is translated into thought by being articulated through the semantic power of *words*. The 'dreamwork', the transformation of a repressed wish into a distorted representation as a dream image, is a manifestation of such a process of translation. For the dream-thoughts that the dream images are transformations of, correspond *exactly* to a verbal formulation of those thoughts – hence the pervasive emphasis in psychoanalytic theory and practice on the distortion of words in jokes and 'forgetfulness'.

In the theory of the psyche presented by Deleuze and Guattari, the unconscious channels sexual energy directly within logical relations without the mediation of words. It produces these relations through a series of logical operations which they call *syntheses*. These syntheses produce a cognitive as well as sexual relation to reality, i.e. something can be known or desired in reality because the psyche has produced a certain kind of relation to that thing. Because energy becomes thought directly, as a result of an activity operating on energy itself without the mediation of words, the psyche is a cognitive apparatus but it is not dependent on a semantic or signifying process. The unconscious does not symbolize. This constitutes a fundamental difference between their theory of the psyche and that of Freudian and Lacanian psychoanalysis. The psyche is not a field of representation but a process of desiring production. This opposition between the psychoanalytic principle of *representation* and this concept of desiring *production* is extended further through an argument derived from Spinoza.

In Deleuze's interpretation of Spinoza, the concept of truth is defined with reference to the metaphysical principle of immanence. Divine nature produces reality, immanently, within itself. Ideas themselves are part of divine nature. To understand the truth of an idea is thus to understand the idea in so far as it is produced within and expresses the cause of divine nature. This principle of immanent production is in *Anti-Oedipus* applied to desire and its relation to social reality: desire is a system of production, producing within a larger system of production that is society. What is produced always simply *is what it is*, that is, energy that circulates, creating connections and enabling further productions.

The paradigm of production is a development of the genetic-expressive method from the Spinoza book: in thought, the correct procedure is to move from a productive principle to what it produces, and not the other way around, from a phenomenon in experience to its conditions. We saw that this opposition distinguished Descartes' reflective method from Spinoza's genetic method. For Deleuze, the principle of production is always defined in relation to a principle of reflection. The principle of reflection states that one begins with what is given in experience, Cartesian ideas, Freudian dreams, and starts reasoning on the basis of these phenomena: is my idea true? What does the dream mean? The productive principle sidesteps this moment of reflection by seeing what is manifest in experience not as a starting point but as the result of a productive principle that can be known independently of these particular effects.

This principle of production leads to a critique of explanatory reductionism in psychoanalysis, the attempt to explain the manifestations of desire with reference to an underlying structure of desire. Both Freud and Lacan elaborate sophisticated reductive models of explanation. Activities and signs are led back to a system of normal behaviour and deviances in Freud or to a dialectic of representation and the non-representable in Lacan. For Deleuze and Guattari, the immanence of desiring production implies that no manifestation of desire carries a signification. Desire simply is what it is; it does not imply or mean, or refer to, some underlying structure that has to be revealed through psychoanalytic interpretation. Thus, the cognitive dimension of desiring production is the immanent logic that it produces, but this logic is not hidden like the dream-thought that has to be uncovered by interpretation, according to Freud. To think is, as Deleuze said in his book on Spinoza, to develop an object in thought. Thought in *Anti-Oedipus* develops the logic of desire.

The opposition from the early work between an immanent field of relations and a representational field of judgement is taken up again in *Anti-Oedipus* and applied to the transformation of desire within the Oedipus structure. Desire thus exists in two modes, either as a direct relation to reality or as mediated through representations of individuals with a definite social identity. This opposition is symmetrical to the opposition between social authority, embodied in the personality structure of the Oedipal subject, and pure desiring production manifest in schizophrenia. The Oedipal subject has an indirect relation to its own desire. Desire is mediated and channelled through an unconscious representation of the child's relation to its mother and father. This representation in turn is conditioned by negation, as the boy's representation of the mother as an object of desire is inseparable from his representation of the mother as a forbidden object of desire. Thus, the boy's own desire becomes closely linked, within his representation of it, to the sanctioning of that desire by the father.

The Oedipal trajectory further consists for the boy in overcoming the hatred he feels towards his father by transforming aggression into identification, overcoming his own inferiority by realizing that he too can be a sanctioning authority, a powerful father and husband, a heterosexual subject. Because of this dynamic of reversal and identification, the boy comes to identify with the sanctioning authority itself, endorsing it to the point of building his own subject position upon it. He defines his relation to the object of desire and his position within social reality upon the negation of his own desire and the parallel identification with a paternal position and figure of authority. It is this profoundly negative model of desire in the Oedipal model which is both praised and criticized in *Anti-Oedipus*: praised as an accurate description of the modern subject, criticized as the celebration of that subject and of its negative self-relation.

The more technical aspects of this critique of psychoanalysis involve a transcendental analysis of the Oedipus complex considered as a structure of representation. The negation of the mother as sexual object presupposes that the mother is identified *as* a mother, i.e. as a certain kind of individual with a precise social identity defined by her position within the family. The negation involved in the representation of the mother as forbidden object involves, on the one hand, an *irrealization* of the object and presupposes, on the other, the notion of a social individual with a definite identity within the family. Desire does not spontaneously relate to parts of reality within a representational grid that would allow it to identify something as an individual with a specific social identity. This is what has to be explained and which psychoanalysis, on the contrary, takes for granted. The mother is identifiable by the unconscious *as mother*, as an individual who is an adult, i.e. who is not a child, who is female and different from the father because the unconscious has learnt to apply a set of logical operations that allows it to *identify* and *differentiate* between individuals. In its logical and cognitive argument, *Anti-Oedipus* undertakes to analyse the dependence of desire upon the Oedipal representation of desire within psychoanalysis, as a *transcendental* problem, centred on the question: how can the psyche be made to operate so that it identifies individuals and differentiates between them according to a principle of social identity? This analysis amounts to explaining how desiring production is Oedipalized, how, in other words, desire comes to function within a grid of representation. Ultimately the account of this process will be historical, but the first step in the argument is logical and transcendental and involves simply the question of how the psyche must function as a cognitive apparatus if it is to identify social individuals and differentiate between them.

The psyche in its primary mode of functioning operates through three syntheses. The first of these is a process of selection called *connective synthesis*. It is the most basic way in which the psyche establishes a relation. In its primary or minimal form, this selection operates upon bodily fluids. Just as many of the societies studied by ethnographers attribute special roles to bodily fluids and excretions, so also are these the primary materials of the psyche in *Anti-Oedipus*. To defecate, urinate or menstruate are actions that embody a logical operation: a stream of some substance is interrupted at certain intervals, thereby a selection is made, and a distinction is established between the stream and the selected part. The psyche produces relations because it can apply this formal operation of cutting into a stream also within other domains.

The connective synthesis manifests itself as a selection which correlates some part of the material world with some part of the body. This relation is called a machine, as in the example of an infant sucking the mother's breast. This situation is described as a cutting machine coupled to a milk-producing machine. The example illustrates several properties of the connective synthesis:

1　The machine forms a *circuit* of desire. The pleasure produced in the infant is inseparable from the concrete process that takes place between the mouth and the breast.
2　The selection of the breast is *self-sufficient* and non-representational. The infant does not need to know who the breast belongs to.
3　The machine is *serial*. The mouth forms one machine, and the breast another, and the fingers which may be holding onto the breast at the same time form yet a third, separate machine.

Desiring production thus works through self-sufficient circuits coupled onto other circuits. Desire works through the particular machines that are available for it without referring to a central instance, such as a subject that would coordinate the machines and express itself through them. Equally, there is no object of desire, for the notion of an object implies temporal continuity and a set of determinations through which it can be identified as an object of a certain kind. Yet a machine needs neither to know what it selects nor whether the machine it is coupled to is of a certain kind or has a definite identity. The immanence of desiring production thus renders the terms of subject and object in their usual sense superfluous.

The second synthesis constitutes a step-up in logical complexity. It is called the *disjunctive synthesis*. The disjunctive relation does not operate directly on a given material as the connective synthesis does. For in order for a disjunction of alternatives to emerge it must first have access to a logical space in which to operate. There must be a medium in which alternatives can co-exist as alternatives. This presupposes a space of coordination within the psyche. This space of coordination is a medium which is not confined within the particularity of individual sensations. It is a moment of *indifferentiation* preceding all articulations of elements into a set of relations. This non-differentiated medium is a transcendental horizon of the psyche, a primary virtual space which must be presupposed before scattered elements can be assembled. This horizon is called the *body without organs*.

The body without organs is further characterized as a surface of inscription. On this surface, sensations are stored and recorded as pure psychic intensities. The disjunctive synthesis records the selections made by the connective synthesis as alternatives co-existing simultaneously in the unconscious. The disjunctive synthesis is thus not exclusive but inclusive; it maintains the alternatives without choosing between them.

When desire runs through these intensities, a part of its energy is as if 'left over' in the psyche. A portion of energy is stored which does not correspond to any particular intensity but to the capacity on the part of the psyche to feel its own intensities, its own sensations. This constitutes the third synthesis, the *synthesis of conjunction*. The synthesis of conjunction produces a subject, an I-function, in which each intensity, each recorded sensation is recognized as belonging to that I. This subject is never assigned a fixed place within the psyche. For it is immanent within the desire that circulates in the disjunctive synthesis, which in turn derives its intensities from the operation of the connective synthesis. Thus, desiring production produces its own subject, but a subject that cannot step outside of production, a subject which is internal to desire. This subject therefore also does not correspond to any individual or personal identity. It is a migrating I-function, a nomadic subject accompanying desire as it passes through the intensities inscribed on the body without organs.

The Paralogisms of Desire

Now, the Oedipal transformation of desiring production consists in the following. Desiring production, which is neither representational nor oriented towards the form of the individual person, becomes moulded within a logical space of representation so that it will direct itself towards whole individuals. For this to be possible, the three syntheses must be transformed so that they no longer operate as *connection, disjunction* and *recognition* but as logical tools for discerning and identifying social individuals.

As we saw, Deleuze and Guattari call the steps in this transformation of the cognitive apparatus of the unconscious, *paralogisms.* Kant uses this term to designate the genesis of an Idea of the self as a spiritual substance. We never actually experience such a Self. Thus, for us to form the Idea of such a substantial self we have to construct it by transforming categories of experience to that which we cannot experience. In a similar way, Deleuze and Guattari claim, the unconscious can learn to apply its syntheses outside of normal desiring production in order to construct a whole individual as object of desire and to identify itself as a socially defined subject.

The paralogism argument accounts for the difference between desiring production and 'Oedipal subjectivity'. It has five parts. In other words, there are five 'paralogisms' or transcendent logical operations within the psyche. Properly speaking, however, not all these paralogisms are in fact mental operations. Only the first three are mental operations, each correlated with one of the syntheses of the unconscious. The other two apply to the personality structure and social identity of the Oedipal subject that is thus constructed.

The first two syntheses of desiring production presuppose each other. The connective synthesis operates on fragments and the disjunctive synthesis of recording constitutes a serial ordering of intensities derived from these fragments. Neither the selection operated by the connective synthesis nor the ordering of intensities are representational so that any one intensity or fragment is made to signify another. In the vocabulary of semiotic codification, the primary processes of the psyche are non-codified. The psyche in its original mode of functioning is a-signifying. It orders brute sensations and thoughts without organizing this material as a language.

The first paralogism consists in transforming the synthesis of connection so that it becomes representational; from simply cutting and connecting, it will operate a categorial distinction between objects within its environment. The category that it learns to employ is that of gender. By implication, the first synthesis thereby also begins to orient itself towards whole individuals as opposed to body parts as only whole individuals can fall within the category of gender. Use of the gender category is, needless to say, an important condition for entry into the Oedipal complex: there can be no rivalry with the father over the mother as sexual object if gender remains unspecific as it does within the primary production of sensation where masculinity and femininity are simply zones of intensity upon the body without organs. The first paralogism introduces a categorial demarcation upon these intensities.

The second paralogism builds on and reinforces the first. It transforms disjunction from being an a-signifying coordination of intensities to being a procedure of logical differentiation. This process of differentiation applies to individuals who are constituted as clearly demarcated and discernible in relation to one another. Disjunction thus moves from being *inclusive* – either A or B or both – to becoming rigid or exclusive – either A or B but not both. The operation of differentiation can now be applied within the category of gender distinction acquired through the first paralogism so that the psyche is now seen to possess the necessary logical operations to produce the Oedipal family representation: you are either a boy or a girl and you are defined in relations to parents who are either father or mother.

The first two paralogisms define the logical presuppositions of Oedipalization (gender specification and differentiation). In the third paralogism, this analysis is continued, but at the same time a different problem is introduced: that of the relationship between social production and desiring production in the constitution of an Oedipal subject.

Within desiring production, the third synthesis produces a subject of sensation, but this subject is not identified as an ideal self or a whole individual. It is an I-function that is immanent within the states of intensity that desire passes through. On the body without organs it holds no fixed position. It is trans-positional and nomadic. The third paralogism transforms this nomadic subject into a subject who is a social self, who identifies itself as belonging to a definite race, group and class.

This process has different components. It originates in desire but it concerns the social determinations of the family. The argument in the third paralogism is that, from the point of view of desire, the family is never a closed or self-sufficient unit. It is always constituted by a relation to social reality as its condition of existence. The psyche works through these social conditions of existence of the family so that the child invests its parents with a definite social identity by locating the family within a social hierarchy. The Oedipus structure is therefore completed when the child, in identifying with the father, also identifies with the father's social identity in terms of class, race, region, etc. Through this process of identification the child ascribes a definite social identity to itself. It takes over the social distinction that defines the group to which the family belongs and applies this to itself, thereby differentiating itself from others. The paralogism of the third synthesis thus transforms a nomadic subject into a socially determined subject. Within the Oedipus structure one learns to say no to one's own desire, one learns to establish sharp logical distinctions and to apply those distinctions to oneself within the social realm. The Oedipus complex is now considered part of the codification of desire by social production through inscription.

The fourth and the fifth paralogisms are not transformations of a particular synthesis, from an immanent to a transcendent use, but characterize the whole Oedipus complex as a logical operation in the psyche. The first three syntheses constitute a representational space within the psyche. This representational channelling of desire signifies, from the point of view of the social control of desire, that it has become receptive of codification. The fourth paralogism makes this process explicit. Social production cannot operate on desiring production directly as a repression of desiring production, or, in other words, for desire to become the object of semiotic codification desire must enter the form of representation. The social repression of desire thus presupposes a transformation of the desiring machine into a structure of representation. The Oedipal complex is this representation. The Oedipus structure thereby functions as a passageway between internal censorship of desire and social control of desire. This also means that the Oedipus structure transforms social repression into a psychological process that consists for the psyche in internalizing political power and refiguring it as an instance of authority and psychic repression within the psyche.

Whereas the fourth paralogism displays the social function of the Oedipus structure, the fifth paralogism serves to close the model of this structure around its own representational status, thereby masking its social origin. In the fifth paralogism, the Oedipus structure is represented to itself as the pure product of a representational relationship between desire and parental figures. The fifth paralogism thus designates the space and function of psychoanalysis within the constitution of the Oedipus complex.

Social Production and Capital

The critique presented through the paralogism argument is situated within a larger, historical and materialist framework that draws indirectly on Marx's theory of production. Whereas Marx's theory, as we saw, is socio-economic, the social theory in *Anti-Oedipus* is genetic and semiotic. It is a theory of how society constitutes a self-generating process of production, called 'social production'. The concept of social production has in common with Marx's economic theory of production that in both cases the concept of production is a fundamental genetic principle that precedes and ultimately accounts for the relationship between individuals and society.

For Marx, the process of production has a definite historical character, characterized by a particular mode of production, such as feudalism or industrial capitalism. Each mode of production establishes a specific division of labour, and as a consequence particular relations between classes. Deleuze and Guattari do not follow Marx in proposing a structural model of this kind. Social production does not differentiate between groups or types of activity but encompasses the whole social realm in so far as the relationship between desire and power is coextensive with social reality.

However, their account of social production under capitalism follows Marx's theory of 'capital' quite closely. For Marx, 'capital' is the outcome of an historical and economic process of development. It is a structural concept characterizing a whole set of relationships within a particular mode of production. The first part of *Das Kapital* is an attempt to define the concept of economic value within the capitalist mode of production by examining various stages in the generation of wealth, beginning in manufacture, continuing with trade and ending in financial investment. This development is characterized by a movement of increasing abstraction: capital itself is defined as abstraction from any material substance; it is the ideal manifestation and circulation of economic value detached from the bonds of land, social obligations and political authority.

For there to be capital, there must first of all be commodity production: goods must be manufactured with the purpose of being sold. A farmer who makes tools for his own use does not produce commodities. Second, the exchange of commodities must have acquired the level of abstraction that is implied by money. A barter economy does not identify the money form as a formal equivalent of all commodities independently of their individual qualities. Third, the process of economic exchange must become independent of the immediate context of consumption. This third level of abstraction allows capital to come into play as a process of self-generating wealth. As capital, wealth is by definition in circulation. In so far as capital is in circulation, it is independent of any individual circumstance, whether a person, a concrete portion of wealth – such as a factory – or a nation-state. Capital is by itself international.

This transgressive and abstractive dynamism of capital implies a non-conventional form of causality. In one sense, capital is the *product* of capitalist activity, just as, in one sense, labour is the source of wealth and production, but according to the economic totality in which capital becomes what it is, *capital is its own causal principle*. It is the action of capital itself which generates a movement of ever increasing capital accumulation. This causal principle is the *logic* of capital; it is a drive towards accumulation and growth internal to capital itself as capital 'wants' and pushes towards ever more production and circulation.

Capital is thus the ultimate subject of capitalism, in so far as capital contains the principles that workers and capitalists must conform to when they enter the market – the worker to sell his labour force, the capitalist to derive profit from this labour force. This abstract and autonomous logic of capital is made possible by the abstract and formal nature of all the elements of capitalist production. For the constituents of capital – labour, commodities, money – are all defined by formal equality. Capital itself as the process and logic of accumulation presides over the entire set of equivalents within production and exchange and thus constitutes the ultimate definition of value. Capital is therefore the end point of a historical abstraction process. It defines value abstractly and it is itself an abstract reality, different from any concrete portion of wealth.

Historically, the abstract movement of capital under capitalism entailed a breakdown of those social and political bonds that held feudal society together. For Marx, capitalism is therefore politically ambiguous. It produces freedom from feudal bonds but is also a source of new kinds of subjection and exploitation. This ambivalence is at the centre of Deleuze and Guattari's analysis of modern society and of the subject emerging within that society. They take over Marx's theory of capital as the outcome of a historical process of abstraction from material attachments and conventional forms of authority. They call this process *deterritorialization*, indicating a movement of detachment from any dependence on a particular piece of land, or national frontier. The deterritorializing force of capital is a dynamic principle that distinguishes modern industrial societies from all previous societies. Capital deterritorializes political and social power, i.e. authority. It undermines the power of the state apparatus and transfers the origin of social production from agencies of power to the delocalized logic of capital. It introduces an abstract logic of exchange and equivalence as the completely formal – they say 'axiomatic' – set of principles determining all activities within the social realm. In order to see the full implications of this process in their social theory we must first look at their conception of history.

Universal history delineates three ways in which desiring production is organized within social production. The end point of history is the point where desiring production is separated from social production, due to the erosion of conventional social authority under capitalism and to the autonomy of the individual within the bourgeois family.

Each period is further characterized by a specific type of social production. Social production is the articulation of social relations according to a given principle of power and distribution. This principle is inscribed on a surface of sense called the *socius*. The socius is a body of inscription analogous to the body without organs within desiring production. The semiotic part of the theory lies in the claim that a part of the economy that circulates in economic production and social relations is inscribed on the socius as the origin of power and wealth. This inscribed origin is then manifest within social life as authority, as the 'semi-divine' source of production. Power only becomes binding as authority when it is inscribed in this way on the socius.

In the simplest type of society, the so-called barbaric society, the socius is the earth. This is a tribal society with no central state that would regulate the relationships between tribes. In such societies, communication *between* tribes is an essential feature of the social life *within* the tribe. The politics of these societies consists in an articulation of relations between tribes *in relation to relations of power* within the tribe. Social production is thus a relation between relations. The alliances created by the circulation of women in inter-tribal marriage are organized in relation to the blood relations of lineage.

The articulation of these two relations with one another is what has to be inscribed as the origin of power and status. Social production in the tribal society is the generation of status and power through the coordination of alliance and lineage. The social inscription of this production takes the form of ritual. The earth as socius is not inscribed directly, however, but the material substance of the tribe, the collective body of its members, is treated as the continuation of the earth, as a material ground of inscription. Rituals then inscribe on the body of the tribe members the relationship between alliance and lineage. Thereby, the tribe members enter a direct relation to social production. Social production inscribes itself as violence and writing on the body without the mediation of social institutions and without the coordinating influence of a state.

Deleuze and Guattari emphasize that the primary form of politics before the invention of statehood is one that is not regulated within a contractual system of reciprocal relations but depends instead on a brute form of power politics. For a contractual system implies a type of representation and codification of the social realm of a higher order of abstraction than the direct, physical inscription of the socius that characterizes the pre-state society. Such a representation presupposes statehood. The invention of the state thus signifies the creation of an indirect, representational mode of governance and control of the social realm, enabling a formal regulation of social activity on the plane of bureaucracy. On the level of alliance, which marks the passage from a system of blood to a social system and which is therefore the crucial feature of social production, the surplus value of code has an essentially, and necessarily, non-reciprocal character, according to Deleuze and Guattari.

This argument is formulated in direct opposition to the anthropologist Marcel Mauss, a student of Durkheim. Mauss and Durkheim were concerned to argue that the foundation of the social bond is rational in a double sense, as being both scientifically intelligible and grounded in rational collective behaviour. For Mauss, this meant that the practice of aggressive gift-giving (potlach), which is one of the best-known instruments for generating prestige in pre-state societies, was a proto-form of a contractual, hence, reciprocal and rational social relationship. As Mauss says: 'The obligation to reciprocate constitutes the essence of the potlach, in so far as it does not consist in pure destruction.'[6] For Deleuze and Guattari, this is a very important theoretical issue. For if the legal representation of society, in which society is seen to constitute a space of collective, reciprocal rationality, can be applied to societies without a state, this representational view of the body politic will have become naturalized. They argue against this position in the version given of it by Lévi-Strauss in his theory of marriage alliance. They argue that so-called 'exchangism', a Maussian conception of alliance as a reciprocal relationship, distorts the nature of social production in a pre-state society.

Against this 'exchangist' view they argue that in tribal societies the social inscription, i.e. the generation of surplus value of code is based not on reciprocal relationships but on asymmetric, political and economic relations epitomized by the notion of *debt*: The rationale of potlach is to render others indebted to one. This is not simply a demonstration of power, but the constitution of a semiotic value, a surplus value of code, since the debt relation is doubly signifying: it signifies a social relation and it signifies wealth and power. Reciprocity, on the other hand, is only possible within a regime of representation for it requires the semiotic homogenization of the social realm. Tribal society, by contrast, is the exact opposite; it is the foundation of the socius on asymmetry as the basis for surplus value of code. The passage from the first to the second period, from pre-state to state societies is thus marked by an increased level of abstraction, a homogenization of the social realm from the point of view of a centre imposing a representational system of regulation.

This new regime, which they call the 'despotic regime', they see as characteristic of archaic states. The archaic despotic state is the state that realizes the very principle of statehood in its most pure and radical form. Despotic rule is characterized by an extreme centralization of power and government, enacted through registers and protocols with which the state surveys the activities of the ruler's subjects. The state symbolically and effectively absorbs society and dominates it. Power is bundled in a point which is represented within society as its unifying centre. Whereas the earlier social formation controlled desire by the codification implied by ritual and marriage without any central authority to coordinate this codification, despotic society emerges through an act of coordination of pre-existing codes. Deleuze and Guattari call this process 'overcoding': on top of existing social rules the despot establishes his own system of centralized legislation. Whereas power in the earlier society was instable, power is now scrupulously maintained.

By centralizing power in the figure of the despot, this type of society produces a new political and psychological category, namely, authority. Whereas the clan elder would have status or prestige as a direct result of social interaction, the despot has a claim to respect that transcends any particular rule or interaction. The figure of the despot thereby constitutes a form of authority which is not derived from any concrete process of social exchange.

In the barbaric society no bureaucracy can fix or impose the meanings of rules and rituals. The meaning effects produced by a ritual are instead both direct and polysemic. They are part of how society works but do not require a specific interpretation. What is inscribed on the human body is not the equivalent of a spoken word and what is seen in a ritual is not the translation of a specific rule. Despotic rule, on the other hand, introduces administrative require-ments of transparency: Rules must be understood in order to be applied. The administrative procedures originating within the des-potic regime require a strict equivalence between writing and speech so that the direct visual encounter with the thing talked about, as in rituals, is rendered superfluous.

Under the despotic regime, desire is thus separated from its direct investment in social production through the representational 'over-coding' of social exchange and desiring production. In tribal societies, ritual would establish an identity between desire and social production, whereby desire invests the ritual at the same time as the ritual seals the belonging of the individual to the social body. This direct process of inscribing desire onto the socius is rendered superfluous by the representational machine of despotic codifica-tion. There is therefore in the despotic state no *direct* manifestation of social production and no immediate encounter between desire and the process that codes it. The direct relation between power and desire is replaced by the mediation of representation. Over-coding means that desire is inscribed onto the socius through a semiotic system of one-to-one or 'bi-univocal' representation.

Now the transition from the despotic state to a capitalist state entails an even higher order form of abstraction. Whereas the rep-resentation of over-coding is still in the service of a state apparatus, the completely formal process of abstraction that Marx theorized as the logic of capital is not bound by any form of social authority or state power. Society is no longer held together by material bundles of social power. Society itself becomes a fluid process of exchange. This leaves open the question of how modern capitalist societies control themselves, how they impose order on their subjects, in short, how they control desire. This is where the process of Oedi-palization shows its historical importance: For Oedipalization is the internalization of authority, creating a subject that obeys itself, by learning to negate its own desire, rather than an external law. Thus, the Oedipus complex, as it is imposed on the psyche through the paralogisms, reterritorializes the authority that capital has deterritorialized.

The Politics of Subjectivity

The central political thesis in *Anti-Oedipus* is that the separation between the logic of capital and socio-political authority, a separation which seems to grant unlimited freedom to the individual subject, is in fact accompanied by a previously unseen collaboration of desiring production in the construction of authority and social control. The political and economic separation of the two regimes of production, produced by the deterritorializing logic of capital, is thus, paradoxically, combined with their identification on the level of desire. In capitalism, the semiotic codification of production is carried out to a very large extent by the individual subject through the Oedipal structure.

This paradox of a freedom leading to greater servitude within industrial modernity is a very common theme in post-Nietzschean social theory. Foucault's theory of the disciplinarian society and Adorno and Horkheimer's dialectic of enlightenment are versions of this argument. The originality of *Anti-Oedipus* thus does not lie in having identified this ambivalent nature of freedom in modern societies but in the theory of desire and power which justifies this thesis in their argument. For within the context of desiring production and its relation to social production the problem of political freedom is primarily sexual, arising from the use we make of libidinal energy. Political freedom is won or lost at an unconscious libidinal level before we come to be active as conscious cognitive and decision-making subjects.

The universal history in *Anti-Oedipus* is the genealogy of the Oedipal formation of self-imposed authority. The historical thesis is that the Oedipus structure as a system that controls desire is universally possible but that it can only unfold under capitalism. The genealogical method entails a layering of historical conditions within the present. This means that the origin of the modern, Oedipal subject lies in a series of earlier stages of historical development. For the second, despotic, period develops politically what the Oedipal subject will produce subjectively – namely, *a representational system of authority*. The despot transcends the laws that he imposes. This has the consequence that the semiotic system of over-coding or social representation points to the despot as an ultimate meaning-giver transcending the system that he grounds. This transcendence within a system of representation corresponds to the modern Oedipal subject as theorized by Jacques Lacan. In Lacanian psychoanalysis, the subject can only enter language, constitute itself within the symbolic order, by confronting paternal authority which founds and transcends this symbolic order. The genealogical truth of Lacan's theory is therefore not universal but historical, according to Deleuze and Guattari. He has accurately revealed what constitutes the misery of the modern human being, i.e. to live under the shadow of authority structures developed at an earlier historical stage, within despotic rule.

However, the central point in the argument – how it is that desire becomes tied to authority under capitalism; in other words, how it is that authority is internalized – is not explained genealogically by the mere survival of the despotic regime of representation. It requires an account of how the relation between desiring production and social production changes in the transition from despotism to capitalism.

Within desiring production, the manifestation of this bond between desire and social production is fear. Despotism produces fear in all its subjects. Fear is the mechanism through which social production enters desiring production in the despotic regime. The Oedipal subject maintains this internalization of social production as fear but changes its object. Since the subject is no longer confronted with despotic authority, *it can now only fear itself.* Isolated from social production by the bourgeois family and the veil of Oedipal representation, it directs its fear towards its own desire in so far as this desire implies a threat to the moral order that the subject has imposed on itself. This dynamic implies the notion of the Oedipal incest as an imaginary transgression which keeps the subject in fear of itself. We may say that this modern Oedipal subject relating to itself and to its desire through imaginary representations is Kant and Sade in one. Within the Oedipal scenario of a repressed, and hence imaginary, incestuous desire for the mother, the subject fears what it represents as a transgression of the law that it has imposed on itself.

This self-repression through fear is, as we saw in the discussion of the paralogisms, identical to the process by which social production inscribes desiring production. We have also seen, on the other hand, that under capitalism there is no direct process of over-coding, no mapping of desiring production onto a centralized socius.

Inscription therefore takes on a paradoxical, we might say, dialectical form. Oedipalization is a representational, and hence inscriptive and codifying, transformation of desiring production which apparently is carried out by the child on itself on the level of unconscious desires and identification (psychoanalytic account). This apparent self-sufficiency of representation is unmasked by the social implications of the paralogism argument: the family is not just the screen onto which the child projects its desires, the stock from which it takes its unconscious representations, but an active social agency of repression, moulding and shaping desiring production in a familial and Oedipal direction. This social-pressure account is only apparent, however. For *Anti-Oedipus* is close to but never identical to a sociological functionalist explanatory framework. In such a framework we would have to say that the family exercises pressure and control over the child in order to provide the state with docile citizens, for example.

Instead, with a dialectical twist, they argue that it is still *desiring production that desires its own repression*. Desiring production is thus the ultimate agent of the repression carried out against it. Only desiring production itself is responsible for its own repression in so far as it is *production* and not a Freudian 'theatre of representation'. The explanatory concept which is here invoked and which is close to but still distinct from the functionalist concept of acting 'in order to' or 'for the sake of' is the concept of 'reterritorialization': the capitalist state reterritorializes desiring production which has been deterritorialized through the destruction of the despotic regime. Reterritorialization works like libidinal energy in Freud's economic model of the psyche: inscriptive energy, and hence the social responsibility for the codification of desiring production, flow from the state into desiring production itself under capitalism. This process is what constitutes the modern liberal subject, a subject that is free and autonomous precisely because it has taken over from the state the responsibility to control itself.

Capitalism erodes political authority and makes the state into a regulator of capital. Power becomes decentred and is ultimately identical to capital itself, but at the same time capital does not exist in a political vacuum. It requires a state which has preserved some of its former, despotic traits. At the same time as capitalism depends on the state, the state will seek to counter the deregulatory effects of capitalism. It will seek to hedge in what capital dissolves. It will institute laws, barriers and institutions. It will try to define through laws and sanctions what can circulate, where and when. This process is a return to a form of codification, but because it happens in response to capitalism, it does not have the same function as despotic rule. It is the attempt to wrest some power away from capitalism by creating pockets of control, setting up territorialities. The capitalist state is a reterritorializing state.

Modern capitalist societies produce a highly ambivalent form of political power. On the one hand, wealth is concentrated in few hands, within alliances between the state and private capital. State power and economic power are dependent on each other and consolidate each other. The interests of big industry coincide with the interests of the state. On the other hand, the logic of capital is to liberate productive energy from social customs and political power. Thus, capitalist society contains the germs of an inner conflict between state power and capital. The state is dependent on social, legal and geographic unity. Capital undermines these unities since, in principle, it is a drive towards limitless accumulation irrespective of any social or geographical limitation. The capitalist state harbours a secret fear of this conflict with capital as untrammelled energy. This fear pushes the state towards strengthening those social forms of authority that capitalism would otherwise undermine. The logical outcome of the capitalist state is therefore the fascist state, the state in which the economy has been fully re-appropriated by the state apparatus, in which production is directed towards the ultimate aims of the state, i.e. the consolidation of its own military power. This ambivalence of the capitalist state is not predictable. No one can foresee when the system will flip, when the liberation of capital will turn into a re-affirmation of the state. This ambivalence introduces indeterminacy into the core of the capitalist system.

Universal history is a movement of increasing semiotic abstraction. In the capitalist regime, meaning is deterritorialized together with capital. Capital entails a form of abstraction in which equivalence marks no hierarchy between form and content. If I buy a hat for 100 słoty, it is not clear what in this transaction would be 'form' and what would be 'content'. The relation of equivalence between money and object is formal rather than representational. Money has no content, only exchange value. With this deterritorialization of the sign, capital implies a new semiotic regime. *Bi-univocation* was the operation that the despot's bureaucracy applied to archaic social rules. The vivid and polysemic reality of ritual was replaced by unambiguous one-to-one relationships within an order of representation. This semiotic regime of representation survives in capitalism at the level of desire in Oedipalization. Desiring production which is in itself non-representational is reterritorialized within the representational space of the Oedipus structure. Capitalism itself, however, is a deterritorializing force which threatens to erode the boundaries of this semiotic regime and thereby destroy the representational space of the Oedipal subject. This possibility is embodied in *Anti-Oedipus* by the figure of the schizophrenic which obeys the same deterritorializing principles as capital. The schizophrenic deterritorializes the sign from its material reference and the subject from its social identity. (It is commonly believed that the mental illness known as schizophrenia often involves a particular kind of language disorder in which language becomes autonomous in relation to experience.)

Schizophrenia constitutes a bridge between social production and desiring production within capitalism. It is, on the one hand, the positive limit or utopian possibility of desire within capitalism, desire existing in a pure state, unlimited by social forces. On the other hand, schizophrenia is also a product of capitalism, the form that capitalism assigns to its own dissolution, the figure of its inner fear. Schizophrenia is therefore produced by capitalism in the form of individuals incapable of functioning within the capitalist system.

The same ambivalence as exists in the capitalist state between deterritorialization and reterritorialization holds on the level of the *individual subject*. The figure of the schizophrenic as a point of absolute deterritorialization is difficult to separate from the figure of the paranoid. Indeed, in psychiatry, the two terms of paranoia and schizophrenia have often been used in conjunction. According to *Anti-Oedipus*, the paranoid is someone who, by rejecting the primary recording of desiring machines on the body without organs, seeks not to enter desiring production. If this primary rejection is transferred onto the state, the paranoid desires that the state as an agent of control represses his own desiring production. Paranoia is thus potentially fascist whereas schizophrenia, if realized as a political practice, would be revolutionary. The revolutionary schizophrenic impulse would inject desiring production directly into social production, thereby breaking the veil of representation that isolates desiring production from social production within the Oedipus structure.

However, in tension with this rather optimistic view of desire as a revolutionary force embodied in the schizophrenic, Deleuze and Guattari present a more dystopian, not to say paranoid, understanding of how desire relates to the capitalist state. The state appears here as an enormous political, scientific, economic and military apparatus, an inescapable net of interdependent institutions that no one can ultimately escape from. This overwhelming scope of state power is another source of ambiguity on the level of the individual and its relation to the state:

> Gregory Bateson begins by fleeing the civilized world, by becoming an ethnologist and following the primitive codes and the savage flows; then he turns in the direction of flows that are more and more decoded, those of schizophrenia, from which he extracts an interesting psychoanalytic theory; then, still in search of a beyond, of another wall to break through, he turns to dolphins, to the language of dolphins, to flows that are even stranger and more deterritorialized. But where does the dolphin flow end, if not with the basic research projects of the American army, which brings us back to preparations for war and to the absorption of surplus value.[7]

The question which *Anti-Oedipus* raises and does not quite answer is then: what are the possibilities of resistance to capitalism's colonization of the globe and of the mind?

Do artists or philosophers, journalists or intellectuals have any role to play? The socius invades desire and desire invests the socius in different ways, but in this process of mutual determination can arenas of action emerge that are less predetermined? Can there be modes of action or processes of change that are not defined either as a contribution to the logic of capital, or as participation in a process of *reterritorialization,* or as a complete dissolution of the self in schizophrenia? The profound ambivalence of capitalism and desire makes it difficult to articulate any such space of agency or creation. For we cannot know in a given case what has a schizophrenic (revolutionary) and what has a paranoid (fascist) potential. As for capitalism itself, 'it is impossible to separate deterritorialization and reterritorialization from one another, they are involved, one within the other, and are like the two sides of the same process'.[8]

Because of the all-encompassing reach of the Oedipal process, *Anti-Oedipus* bars the way to any pragmatic strategy for resistance to capitalism. The dialectic of repression and desire that Oedipalization produces leaves no conceptual space outside this process from which one could resist it. In Oedipalization we become complicit in our own subjection at the unconscious level of desiring production.

We learn, through Oedipalization, to inscribe the negation of our own life force into the very basic categories that we employ to situate ourselves within the capitalist social order, the categories of the individual subject and object. The only alternative to this process of participation in subjection is a very radical rejection of this representational structure within the psyche. The two versions of this rejection, paranoia and schizophrenia, and their corresponding political expressions, fascism and revolutionary politics, are posed in opposition both to the liberal Oedipal subject and to the capitalist order of which this subject is a central figure. Now, the opposition to Oedipal subjection posed by these two other forms of desire is so radical that one cannot see how there could be a transition between them and the Oedipal subject. In other words, it is not clear how the Oedipal subject could escape its own Oedipal structures once they are in place. It is not clear, for instance, how the free and uncodified energy of a nomadic subject could, surreptitiously, be infused within Oedipal normality.

The model is therefore dualistic and Romantic in its idealization of a primary force of alienated desire. This Romanticism is tied to the presentation of a subject that is so radically immanent within its own circuits of desire that it can hardly be given the political task of challenging existing forms of power. Under capitalism, power acquires a systemic quality. Processes of deterritorialization and reterritorialization nourish each other to the point of becoming indistinguishable. It is difficult to see how the radically immanent nomadic-schizophrenic subject could be able to make a difference in the face of this systemic power. The critique of Oedipal subjectivity, for all its sophistication, thus leaves an issue of subjectivity unresolved, namely the issue of how agency can be construed outside of the representational relation to the world, how, in other words, it is possible to construct a rigorously immanent subject which is at the same time active rather than simply alienated or excluded, like the schizophrenic locked up in the asylum.

It is the project of *A Thousand Plateaus* to construct such an immanent alternative to representational subjectivity. With *Anti-Oedipus*, therefore, a certain critical project has played itself out, the thorough critique of the modern autonomous but self-oppressing individual subject. This critique has left the task of constructing an alternative to the subject that has been criticized. *A Thousand Plateaus* continues the critique of the subject and of representation, but now within a framework that also theorizes the possibility of a different mode of being.

4

Social Ontology

Freedom, Intellectuals and History

A Thousand Plateaus is the sequel to *Anti-Oedipus*. It was published in 1980 but written over a period of years during the late 1970s, often in conjunction with Deleuze's seminars at the University of Vincennes.

Anti-Oedipus had constructed an elaborate critique of the modern subject. It also presented the theory of a different, nomadic subject. This subject would be immanent within the movement of desire. However, the book left undecided whether or how this new nomadic subject could be a subject of political action. It was therefore not clear what would be open to members of modern society as paths of resistance in the face of a seemingly all-encompassing network of social control, since this network had its roots in the normal, Oedipal subject that each of us is, and since the alternative to the self-negation and rigid channelling of desire that defines this subject was the completely other nomadic subject that could only manifest itself at the margins of society, as schizophrenia, as a state of desire that could not be reached through any conscious choice and which in itself would seem to exclude any kind of conscious choice or agency.

The strict duality of the oppressed and self-oppressing Oedipal subject and the alienated freedom of the nomadic-schizophrenic subject raises two different philosophical problems. First, this duality points to a residual Romanticism, a nostalgia for a kind of freedom which the anonymous systems of modernity seem to efface.

As we shall see, this kind of nostalgia has been typical of sociological theories of modernity. If *Anti-Oedipus* does not, quite, espouse this Romantic anti-modernism, it also does not really show a way out of it. That, on the other hand, is one of the deep accomplishments of *A Thousand Plateaus*: it problematizes all the concepts on which this Romantic anti-modernism rests.

Second, the space of political opposition to or contestation of state power seems to be necessarily vacant, since the Oedipal subject will only pursue the trajectory of its own self-negation and the schizophrenic cannot live its nomadism within the social order and is thus condemned to a position of marginalization or exclusion. From this disadvantageous position, it is difficult to see that it will be able to effect or motivate political resistance.

The classical tradition in German sociology, represented by Ferdinand Tönnies and Max Weber, analysed society under the assumption that they were themselves parts of a watershed, witnesses to the beginning of a new kind of society, the modern, impersonal, rationalized society, based on formal procedures, a separation between 'public office' and the person holding the office. Tönnies coined the phrase that came to stand as a motto for the subsequent tradition, the opposition between traditional society or 'Gemeinschaft' which was thought to be ruled by custom and personal bonds, and modern society or 'Gesellschaft' ruled by formalized rules and roles. Weber, for his part, was interested in the impact of these new formal roles upon the individuals who filled them. In studying the relationship between formalized working routines in state administration and large firms, he thought that the motivational structure characteristic of these modern social roles was fundamentally different from the affective bonds and motives for action within more traditional social contexts. For these new roles required a separation between the aims of the institution and the personal aims of the individual. This split left the individual with the feeling of *alienation*, of having lost something of himself. As Weber says of bureaucratic administration: 'The professional bureaucrat is chained to his activity by his entire material and ideal existence. In the great majority of cases, he is only a single cog in an ever-moving mechanism which prescribes to him an essentially fixed route of march.'[1] This feeling of being controlled by a 'system', i.e. by complex chains of causality entirely beyond the control of the individual subject is also a central theme in the social philosophy of Theodor W. Adorno who was inspired by Weber in this respect. For him, art – that is, high art – could hold out a hope of a freedom from this complex web of constraints seemingly determining each aspect of the lives of individual subjects within capitalism. Art would be able to offer an alternative to this structure of determination because the intrinsic indeterminability of art – we cannot causally explain why something is art – makes it resistant to the utilitarian spirit of capitalism: 'In the midst of a world dominated by utility, art indeed has a utopic aspect as the other of this world, as exempt from the mechanism of the social process of production and reproduction.'[2] This analysis of capitalism and modernity entails, and forever repeats, the Romantic figure of an alienated subject of freedom and authenticity, a subject who would be untainted by the processes of 'rationalization' characteristic of modern society. This model is all the more difficult to reject as it has a very strong prima facie plausibility.

As a model of explanation it also relies on certain metaphysical principles. First among these is a conception of society as constituting a closed and coherent structure of determination and domination. We saw that already with the energy model of *Anti-Oedipus*, Deleuze and Guattari refused to establish an explanatory paradigm that would require making a causal map of social processes similar to the structural model of class relations in Marx. Such representations cannot grasp immanently the processes of semiotic production that constitute social reality. In *A Thousand Plateaus*, Deleuze and Guattari pursue this rejection of structural models of explanation even more rigorously.

Second, the sociological critique of modernity presupposes a unitary view of history. Weber may see traces of rationalization in different civilizations and in different periods, but history itself is a movement towards ever greater rationalization. This model of history is, I think, successfully overturned by the genealogical method employed in *A Thousand Plateaus*.

The comparison with Weber and Adorno has uncovered two salient traits of the method and project set forth in *A Thousand Plateaus*. First, it is a critique of explanatory models of society. Second, it seeks to present a genealogical concept of history which differs sharply from the structural and teleological view of history in which it is seen as a movement towards ever greater rationalization. Let us dwell on this difference between, on the one hand, a genealogical and, on the other, a teleological and structural view of history.

The genealogical perspective sees history neither in structural nor in goal-oriented terms, but as the fluctuation of civilizations, corresponding to the prevalence of now one, now another, determining force. In the philosophy of history presented in *A Thousand Plateaus*, there are two sets of forces that pull societies in opposing directions. These polarities are similar but not completely identical. First, all states exercise a pull towards more and more centralization and coordination of social practices through economic systems such as taxation, through conscription, education, and through the attempt to enforce homogenous religious or moral principles. Opposing this movement towards coordination, social reality presents contrary movements of fragmentation: the development of practices or systems that escape coordination, in the realms of science, or sexuality, or religious belief, or through physical or social mobility. Thus, whereas the concept of state coordination seems to conform to the model of rationalization–modernization, the contrary movement of fragmentation does not belong within this model. It is, however, historically obvious that modernity – whether it is seen as a socio-economic development of industry, big cities, a wealthy bourgeoisie, powerful banks, or in more political terms as a process that engenders secularization, democratization, and individualism – in both cases, involves such decentring processes.

Further, the very formality of the two concepts of coordination and decentring makes them designate fluctuations rather than a process that could have a direction. We can say these principles are neutral with respect to the concept of modernity. This neutrality becomes clearer with the second pair of concepts that organize history in *A Thousand Plateaus*: the polarity of *settlers* and *nomads*, issuing in two types of social organization, the state apparatus and what they call the 'nomadic war machine'. The state is identified both with archaic states of 'hydraulic' societies like Ancient Egypt or Mesopotamia and with modern industrial, democratic as well as totalitarian or 'fascist', states. The nomadic war machine is the social realization of a freedom from the cognitive and semiotic principles (the semiotic regime of bi-univocity that we saw in the despotic regime in *Anti-Oedipus*) that are promoted by state organization. This freedom is archaic and primary in that it pre-dates the constitution of the state, but its manifestation is by no means limited to an archaic type of society. The nomadic mode of being consists in cognitive and social principles of relating to the environment (acting, perceiving, organizing relations) outside of the semiotics of codification and representation. The important methodological point about these alternative socio-cognitive principles is that they are trans-historical. They are thus able to migrate from one civilization or type of society to another. The opposition between the state and the nomad is thus not confined to any particular period or type of society.

The relationship between states and nomads is further dynamic. When the state seeks to gain control over the unruly nomadic war machine, both the state and the war machine are transformed. In itself, the war machine is non-representational, whereas the state is identical to a principle of semiotic representation. In their fusion, war itself becomes an object of representation. Thus, the maximum of violence accomplished by war is not prior to the constitution of the state as a condition that the state protects us from. That had been Hobbes' justification for state authority. Rather, war is only possible through the organizational power of the state. Now, this process of transformation can flip and move in the opposite direction, with the nomadic war machine taking over the organization of the state. In this case the state is sidetracked from its normal functioning and becomes completely absorbed in the pursuit of war. The fascist state is just such a state. It subordinates all the actions of the state to the dominant goal of war. The quintessentially modern phenomenon of fascism is thus accounted for within the terminology of state and nomads derived from the very long-term history of civilizations.

Genealogical history is therefore extremely long-term. This long-term perspective also produces a very different conception of the human being from that of the Enlightenment subject of progress or the sociological individual facing modern systems of dominance. It becomes clear in Nietzsche's use of the genealogical method in his *On the Genealogy of Morals,* as we saw in the previous chapter, that the human being is considered from an anthropological perspective, as a natural 'species' or 'human animal' evolving slowly through the history of cultures and societies. Changes in this species history do not occur with the quick pace of industrialization, urbanization, democratization and other modernizing processes but take place across disparate and distant historical epochs and cultures, in other words across successive civilizations. The horizon of intelligibility of the human animal in genealogy is the arc of human civilizations in their succession through the past three or four thousand years. Nietzsche, in his second essay on the origins of moral conscience, conceives the development of morality as the 'learning' on the part of the human animal, of new instincts, namely the non-natural counter-instincts of inhibition and reflexivity. He compares this instinct-history to a change occurring in natural history:

These half-animals who were happily adapted to a life of wilderness, war, nomadism, and adventure were affected in a similar way to the creatures of the sea when they were forced either to adapt to life on land or to perish – in a single stroke, all their instincts were devalued and 'suspended'.[3]

Genealogical history thus conceives of modernity and processes of modernization, a favourite topic of classical sociology, from a perspective that is not derived from the temporal and historical horizon of modernity, and which therefore is also not derived from the experience of living within modernity, the experience of alienation, longing for a lost 'Gemeinschaft' and so on that is a recurrent theme in the German sociological tradition.

Comparing the genealogical method of analysis with the sociological critique of modernity, we can attest to a further difference, now at the level of the mode of address that each of these types of theoretical historical description defines regarding the historical present and regarding its readers.

Within both historical models, the subject of theory entertains a marked and specific relation to the present, but the present is not conceived in the same way. To the sociologist of rationalization, the present is the brink of a future destined to bring ever more modernization, even more rationalization. To the genealogist, by contrast, the present is the end point of a civilization history. Corresponding to this difference, the rationalization model produces the figure of the intellectual as the chief interpreter of the present and of the historical process that it expresses. Genealogy produces the very different figure of a distant and detached observer interpreting the present not as part of a forward-moving process but against the background of a four-thousand year history of variations and fluctuations between opposing tendencies in cultures and societies. Since neither this history nor the societies it runs through possess an intelligible structure that can be summed up and theorized, there is within the genealogical perspective no possible position for the figure of an intellectual, considered as chief interpreter of history.

The intellectual claims to speak on behalf of a community and often, at least implicitly, with a view to future political action. See, for instance, the following passage from Adorno on the notion of 'progress' which he interprets in the light of the Holocaust: 'The forms of humanity's own global societal constitution threaten its life, if a self-conscious global subject does not develop and intervene. The possibility of progress, of averting the most extreme, total disaster, has migrated to this global subject alone.'[4] This global subject corresponds to the figure of the public intellectual. This figure would be a subject mediating between theory and practice, alerting the community to the dangers growing in its midst, pointing to possible futures. This indication of a future horizon of action involves the concept of a community that the intellectual can address and who could become a collective subject of action, a community whose political-spiritual guide the intellectual aspires to be.

The genealogical theorist, on the other hand, is not a subject addressing a community with the view to mediating between theory and practice. His point of view is sceptical. By introducing the long-term historical perspective of civilizations and their successions, he relativizes and questions the self-understanding of the present, its belief, most of all, in the importance of its own beliefs and principles. This scepticism is not, however, dispassionate nor cynical. It does not relativize the principles of progress, democracy and individualism in order simply to affirm a position of indifference to human endeavours. On the contrary, the Deleuzian genealogist defends a cause of freedom, identifies lines of political conflict and potentials for liberation within the constellation of forces that make up contemporary social reality, but these conflicts and potentials are not summarized or amenable to being synthesized into a 'movement of history', or a 'collective political project'. Nor does the genealogist address a political collective.

The commentator John Rajchman accurately diagnoses the original position that Deleuze's thought occupies vis-à-vis political action: 'Often it is a matter of making visible problems for which there exists no program, no plan, no "collective agency", problems that therefore call for new groups, not yet defined, who must invent themselves in the process in accordance with affects or passions of thinking prior to common cognition and its codes.'[5] This reading presents the genealogical theorist as nevertheless being a spokesman of the future, as a liberator who provides the theoretical tools for opening up new ways of thought and life. This is certainly part of the aspiration of *A Thousand Plateaus*, but we shall have to examine in greater detail how theory and practice are related.

There are at least four strands that can be separated at the outset: (1) an ontological-descriptive strand; (2) a genealogical strand; (3) an ethical strand; and (4) an epistemological strand. The ontological strand is a formal description of social reality. The genealogy is a semiotic and historical account of subjectivity and statehood. The ethics is an account of immanent freedom, a freedom that is resistant to external evaluation. The epistemology is a theory of science from the perspective of what we may call 'ontological heterogeneity'.

These four argumentative lines running through the book together compose a complex critique of representation. As an introduction to this critique of representation and before examining each of these dimensions of the critical project in turn, we need, however, to distinguish the social ontology that is at the heart of this critical project from a broad strand of social theory, relying on the representational ontological categories of *individual*, *society* and *state* that *A Thousand Plateaus* seeks to undermine and to replace with a different set of ontological concepts.

The 'Social' and the 'Natural'

Classical sociology and political philosophy have tended to describe social reality in terms of two ontological poles: the *state* or *society* and the *individual*. For Durkheim, society is characterized by the claim of collective norms or 'collective consciousness' on the volition and beliefs of individuals. As a consequence, if this hold on the individual weakens, as Durkheim thinks is the case in modern society, due to the complexity of social relations that he calls 'organic solidarity', there is a danger of social disintegration. The modern condition thus opposes *individualism* and community, or *social cohesion*. As Raymond Aron succinctly puts it: 'Durkheim believes he sees in organic solidarity a reduction of the sphere of existence embraced by the collective consciousness, a weakening of collective reactions against violation of prohibitions, and above all a greater margin for the individual interpretation of social imperatives.'[6] This simple ontological model has an empirical origin. The sociologist observes individuals who occupy different social roles. He then assumes that there must be a sum total of social relations comprising all individuals, thereby arriving at the notion of society.

This dualism of individual and society has a more complex precedent in the tradition of political philosophy as it evolves between Hobbes and Rousseau. If the political problem of early modernity was how to justify the rule of government and the obedience to this rule on the part of individual citizens, the increase of egalitarian ideas in the course of the eighteenth century introduced the notion of a more dynamic and complex relation between state and citizen, requiring the introduction of a third term such as 'society', or the notion of a 'community' uniting all citizens and providing them with the means of realizing their freedom, and not just as in Hobbes with protection from civil war. The historian of political thought Plamenatz explains this development in the area of citizens' rights and entitlements:

> No doubt, most of the great political thinkers before Rousseau had proclaimed a belief in equality, in one form or another; but equality, as they conceived of it, consisted in all men having certain rights, prior to government; rights held to be realized in existing society or to require only an extension of the franchise for their realization. They did not hold, as Rousseau did, that equality, and therefore freedom as well, is impossible except in communities profoundly different, socially as much as politically, from any that have existed.[7]

The gradual development in political philosophy towards an inclusive view of society as a political and even ontological term that both precedes and gives full realization to individual political freedom entails that society is something more than a system of governance and laws, that society in other words, is not simply identical to the state apparatus.

In the political philosophy of Hobbes based on an atomistic ontology of human beings, there is no such third term. Individuals are joined together in a commonwealth under the coercive influence of the ruler whose integrative power consists mainly in maintaining peace and preventing civil discord. The social bond itself is thus difficult to explain within this atomistic paradigm. Attempts at giving a more substantive account of society conceived as a structure that includes and defines its members, both individually and in relation to one another, are articulated in the political philosophy of Rousseau and is continued by Hegel and Marx. The ontological assumption underlying these attempts is still, however, to some extent individualistic. The question posed by social reality is the interdependence of individuals within society even if these individuals, as in Marx, are completely defined by social relations.

A Thousand Plateaus seeks to reopen the question of what constitutes social reality on a basic ontological level, what, in other words, constitutes social being. The dynamic and semiotic theory of production in *Anti-Oedipus* led to the conclusion that the ontological concepts of states, societies and individuals do not refer to anything that would exist prior to and outside of a semiotic process of production. There is a semiotic constitution of reality prior to what appears to be physically or naturally given in experience. This semiotic and genetic theory therefore leads to a very strong anti-empiricism in the field of political thought. Or we might say that the critique of representation that is pursued through this semiotic theory now aims to undermine a series of social ontological categories that have had the authority of natural givens, in sociological and political theory.

A Thousand Plateaus takes this project further, but now the theoretical enquiry moves away from an analysis of power to a description of social reality as a whole. It moves from the question of what constitutes obedience to the question of what characterizes anything that exists in a social realm. The rejection of the state and the individual as primary explanatory and ontological terms flows from the more general epistemological requirement of not reducing social reality, which I shall refer to as 'the social', to a relation existing between previously and independently constituted terms. The social is thus neither an association of individuals nor the domain demarcated by the territorial rule of a given state. Sociality is first of all a dimension of being. But what characterizes this dimension of being which is the social?

To be social is to exist within a certain field of interaction which comprises an extremely wide variety of types of components, but which most importantly exists along the four dimensions of *cognition, space, power* and *history*. To be social is to exist as a mode of *ordering* (cognition), with a determinate relation to an *environment* (space), strengthening, decentring or transforming the *circulation of state power* within a definite realm (power) and participating in a variety of *historical processes* of varying time scales (history).

The social is further characterized by a specific type of *causality* which was introduced in formal terms in *Difference and Repetition* under the name of 'resonance'. This is a kind of causality that differs both from linear efficient causality, where one object has an impact on another in a law-governed manner, and from the kind of structural or systemic causality that is theorized in Marxism and psychoanalysis – the economy of desire and its repression, the logic of capital accumulation. For just as in *Difference and Repetition* it was important to Deleuze to reinterpret classical determinist systems of metaphysics so that they became compatible with chance and indetermination, so here Deleuze and Guattari aim to overturn the structural explanatory methods of the contemporary human and social sciences and replace their notions of causal determination with a completely different kind of determination, which, like the Idea in *Difference and Repetition*, is at the same time the principle that accounts for *individuation*. The determining cause that accounts for individuation is now understood as a resonance between heterogeneous causal series. This means that instead of thinking, as we do in the natural attitude of ordinary experience, that our starting point should be individual objects, events, people, the 'object' of thought is now constituted by constellations of processes and of processes affecting other processes without any such nameable centres that would correspond to the contents of experience.

Further, the category of the social covers any aspect of human activity, it even precedes the distinction between material and mental, for all thoughts and all objects come into being first by being social. The category of the social is therefore neutral in respect to all our categorial divisions of society. There are, in other words, no categorial limits that can hedge in the movement of interaction and resonance that constitute social processes. This open-endedness of causal determination and interaction produces a strong degree of *indeterminacy*. Within this indeterminacy there are potentials for freedom and change – not a freedom represented within a subjective consciousness as its power of choice, not, that is, a freedom entailed by individual or collective consciously chosen action, but a freedom from linear causal determination, a freedom to develop unpredictably.

At the same time as being all-encompassing, the category of the social is not itself a being. There is no one, large entity which may be called society. The social exists as heterogeneous processes and clusters of relations. The resonance or interaction implies that beings of very different kinds influence each other simultaneously. We are unable to represent this interaction by dividing each of its components into categories that would be homogenous for all beings since causal determination and resonance travel across all such categorial divisions. Determination has become *transcategorial*.

It would be impossible to overstate the implications of this new ontology for how we may think of ourselves, of history and of social processes.

Formal Ontology and Social Processes

A Thousand Plateaus engages in a debate with all the human and social sciences and constructs, in the course of this discussion, a general and formal analysis of social formations, relations of power and the types of subjectivity that can emerge under different historical conditions. This analysis is both broader and yet more fragmented than the theory of desire and the state in *Anti-Oedipus*. Instead of constructing one unified theory, Deleuze and Guattari now write a series of relatively independent texts on apparently very different topics. However, while these texts do cover a large range of themes, they are at the same time all concerned with a narrow set of epistemological and metaphysical problems, regarding the nature of order in thought and in society.

A Thousand Plateaus is constructed as a vast epistemological discussion and critique of contemporary human and social sciences. From this critical discussion Deleuze and Guattari derive a description of the whole of human and social reality. The argumentative thrust of the book lies in the structure of this description. The term 'plateau' is neutral with respect to the distinctions between thought and material reality, and between culture and society. This indicates that the book does not have a clear and well-defined object. It does not fit into any existing discipline of science or conform to any particular branch of philosophy. It is, in a sense, a *book about everything*. It is both all-encompassing and open-ended. It covers a wide range of activities, cultural practices, and forms of social organization, ranging from perception and sexuality, music and literature to a discussion of social micro-interaction and the genesis of statehood. However, all these activities, practices and forms of organization are analysed as processes organized according to the same formal principles. This social theory also produces a new critique of representation. For all thought is now seen as a social practice taking place within a force field composed of other social practices.

Thought thus interacts directly with its social environment; it does not belong to a closed realm of representation or subjectivity. Within this social theory of thought, power is in turn internal to the production of thought.

Anti-Oedipus argued that desire is complicit in its own suppression. This argument is now generalized. Thought is now actively participating in its own imprisonment within the grids of representation and subjectivity. The main lines of division that are put in question in *A Thousand Plateaus* are those between thought and reality and between what is individual and what is collective. On the level of the distinction between *thought* and *reality*, the book argues that thought is real, both as a process and as a 'form of content' and that social reality cannot exist independently of the thoughts that it generates and that it embodies through social practices and modes of organization. On the level of the distinction between the *individual* and *society*, it seeks to demonstrate that the same processes run through groups and individuals and that what we take to be a self-conscious subject, an economic agent, an individual speaker, a political citizen or any other figure of the individual are nothing but particular compositions of social energy and power.

The ontology of *A Thousand Plateaus* is entirely formal, constructed around geometrical and geological concepts such as lines, planes, strata. These abstract spatial concepts circumscribe reality, and predominantly social reality, as a composition of processes. The advantage of this abstractly formal vocabulary is that it indicates the material conditions of composition of any being without proposing a model of what it is to be or suggesting that reality has to conform to our representations of it, as in the Aristotelian notion of the 'thing'.

In order to account at the same time for the existence in social reality of systems that seem severely to limit the scope of what there can be, systems that create order within practices of thought and in social practices generally, Deleuze and Guattari oppose two general formal principles: the centralizing principle of the *point* and the a-perspectival principle of the *line*. The line is a compositional principle that has no beginning, centre or end, no ideal viewpoint from which it is to be conceived. The point, by contrast, is the principle of a functional, hierarchical order that has to be conceived from one ideal point of view, namely that point that is indicated by the 'point'.

In any activity of thought, a struggle thus takes place between two kinds of forces. The one pole is a centralizing, hierarchical force that seeks to create stable relations and to represent the world according to these relations. The opposing pole is a non-linear and self-decentring form of organization that can be found in both nature, art and social practices. We recognize the opposition from *Anti-Oedipus* between the controlling power of social machines and the decentring productivity of desiring machines, but in *A Thousand Plateaus* the forces of order and the forces of destabilization manifest themselves *on the same level*, namely, within each practice and each string of thoughts.

Nevertheless, as in the case of the Oedipal subject, rigid social structures have become a historical and social reality. The realization of hierarchical and functional relations within social reality corresponds to the historical development and expansion of state rule. The state is the origin of a principle of governance of the entire social realm exercised through a structural mode of representation, coordination and organization. The state therefore is not just a centre of power but a principle of governance through which power is exercised. The state is not an entity or a thing which could be symbolized as a kind of individual or structure. The state only exists in action, as a principle of statehood. This concept of statehood is both political and epistemological and it is both simultaneously. The state is a type of power which organizes the social field according to structural relationships. This also means that any structural mode of thinking contributes to the expansion of the state.

In order to develop an alternative to structural and hierarchical thought, *A Thousand Plateaus* develops the concept of the *rhizome*: the term 'rhizome' originally refers to a widely spreading tree root. Here the concept of the rhizome is an ordered set of relations in which each element relates to every other, without any hierarchical, functional or centralized order being imposed on these relations. This rhizomatic principle of fluid systems and relations now opposes the organizing principles of state rule, as immanence opposes transcendence. For the semiotics of the state always consists in representing relations according to a central and hierarchical viewpoint that is external to the set of relations that is to be represented. Rhizomatic relations on the other hand are rigorously immanent. To think the rhizome thus requires the method of participation or development that Deleuze characterized in *Spinoza and the Problem of Expression*. This immanence entails that nothing we may say about a rhizomatic process, no list of attributes we may ascribe to it, would ever be able to define that process. A rhizomatic process further consists of partial processes which are not integrated within a structure, and the course of which cannot be predicted from a knowledge of the causes that influence the process. The rhizomatic process is epistemologically immanent in that it excludes an external definition of its course of development. Ontologically the rhizomatic process is characterized by not possessing a reproducible structure of relations.

Obvious examples of immanent processes would be arts which are not codified in writing. Their own favourite example is nomadic warfare. This example underscores another difference between the rhizome and the state. The state is a principle of appropriation and codification. Statehood is the exercise of power through the semiotic process that in *Anti-Oedipus* was called 'over-coding'. Over-coding designates a particular semiotic regime of bi-univocal, or one-to-one, relationships between elements so that a practice can be adequately represented in thought or language. A legal system, a system of taxation, formal rules of warfare obey the semiotic of over-coding. Statehood manifests itself through over-coding and it is through the extension of over-coding to ever larger areas of social reality that the state grows.

The concept of immanence is developed and specified further through the ontological concept of composition. Social interactions and social institutions are not primarily structures conforming to a model, but singular compositions of forces that can only be thought from the inside. *A Thousand Plateaus* is thus a formal theory of social composition. This notion of composition leads us back to the difference between representational and genetic principles of thought and explanation. Representational thought assumes that beings exist as individual things which are identifiable as each belonging to a certain kind. Further, it assumes that what happens to the thing is observable and causally explicable.

The genetic principle is opposed both to the notion of observable traits and to the principle of causal explanation, whether this causal explanation would follow a modern scientific model of empirical laws describing phenomena or the older Aristotelian model of essential properties and final causes. For what determines and individuates processes is a composition of causes which is neither observable nor contained within a definition of these processes.

Any 'object' is a cluster of relations conditioned by a composition of determining forces and processes of different kinds. It exists within an environment which is itself composed of a multiplicity of forces and determining processes. We can therefore not isolate within this cluster an individual thing and ascribe to it a series of events which we then set out to explain. To think an 'object', i.e. to think any feature of reality, is to develop it genetically, to reproduce in thought the composition of forces and determining principles that condition and determine it. *A Thousand Plateaus* applies this genetic principle to all features of social organization including the human 'subject'.

The formal starting point of their method is the concept of multiplicity. A multiplicity is an indeterminate 'group' defined formally as *a capacity to be affected* prior to the elements that it will consist of. The multiplicity develops consistency, becomes something specific and determinate, through the forces that work on it and within it. When a multiplicity is affected it is organized as a set of relations. The ontology put forward in *A Thousand Plateaus* is thus organized as a gradual specification and differentiation of 'multiplicities'. The argument moves from the completely indeterminate concept of multiplicity through different types of social relations and culminates in a concept of complex causal interaction which they call the *abstract machine*. A multiplicity is the most basic element of being, a something which can be affected by forces. An abstract machine is a coordination of heterogeneous causal series, like the field of resonance in *Difference and Repetition*. Social life unfolds between these two orders of determination, the indeterminate capacity to be formed, which is the multiplicity, and the specific determination of series through one another which is the abstract machine.

This ontology is formal in two senses. First, it is expressed in a quasi-mathematical vocabulary, which gives precedence to relations over the beings which are related. Second, this theory of relations, of how they are formed and how they dissolve, is indifferent to the type of being that it is applied to and is then only in a second step applied to social being. Thus we encounter here the kind of philosophical abstraction that in *Difference and Repetition* was theorized through the concept of the third synthesis of repetition.

The third synthesis of repetition produces an absolutely formal process of thinking that does not, in any way, derive its categories from lived experience. The quasi-mathematical vocabulary used to describe social being in *A Thousand Plateaus* pursues this same ideal of abstraction: in order to make sure that one is not prejudiced by the ontological categories entailed by experience one has to produce an absolutely abstract conceptual language to describe social reality – including experience, but experience seen genetically according to its own immanent process of being, and not according to how we represent experience to ourselves from within that experience.

The determination of a multiplicity takes the form of a double articulation into two levels of ordering. Originally used in linguistics to distinguish the organization of language by sound and meaning, the term is used by Deleuze and Guattari to contest the representational Aristotelian ontology of things defined by their essential properties, which is an ontology of one single articulation. The principle of double articulation implies that there are different ordering processes taking place simultaneously within the same being but at different 'levels'. These levels are related as different types of organization. The difference between these two levels of organization is also determined, in part, by different ways of relating to the environment, by having more or less rigid borders, more or less extensive interaction with surrounding beings.

The first level of articulation is a dynamic interaction of simple elements which they call a *molecular* organization. The second level is an ordering according to kinds and categories, which they call *molar* organization. The composition of these two ordering principles forms a *stratification*.

The stratification is undermined by *deterritorializing* forces which may undo it. These forces constitute a *line of flight* affecting a whole stratification or 'assemblage' of stratifications. We thus have four ontological categories defining the formal properties of any determined multiplicity:

1 *molar* categorization;
2 *molecular* dynamics;
3 *deterritorializing* forces that run through both levels of organization;
4 *assemblages* of stratification comprising all three levels of organization and disorganization.

A morphological analysis of society must articulate social being as determined multiplicities according to their double articulation, relations to an environment and deterritorializing factors. To account for events or processes by invoking structures such as class, personality, culture or family is to overlook the double articulation of any stratified being as both molecular and molar, thereby missing the way that any event or process is involved in several levels of reality at once. This does not mean that social life is without order, only that this order involves intersecting layers of organization. Classical sociology seeks to account for social life in terms of underlying principles, such as rational interest, shared norms or principles of organization which make behaviour rationally intelligible. The geological and mathematical terminology of multiplicity and stratification highlights different, non-reductive organizing features of social life.

The primary formation within social reality is the composition of forces that they call an 'assemblage'. The French word that 'assemblage' translates is *agencement*, a term that has a connotation of agency. The assemblage is thus a composition that acts. It occupies the position of a subject in social space but is not defined by self-consciousness. It is an organization of power within a particular medium or stratum. Within the *agencement* a heterogeneous set of forces are assembled so as to produce a specific agency and a particular use of power.

An assemblage exists within, as well as consists of, various strata. A stratum is a field of interaction and development establishing its own porous borders with the environment and with other strata. The geological terminology of strata and stratification indicates that processes are defined by a sort of location. They are the results of force compositions and these compositions must have a location. The stratum is where they take place. It is a layer of relative order. These layers are not identical with physical beings, i.e. the borders of a stratum are not the borders of perceivable objects: a stratum may be relatively small, part of a cell in a body, or relatively large, a dialect spoken in a particular region or the circulation of wealth within a company. Its borders are particular to each stratum and therefore not necessarily spatial and appearing on the outside of objects.

Strata and assemblages are organized and operate according to semiotic principles of order that they apply to their environment. They also, however, produce sense, surfaces of inscription existing as social reality, as the ideal and signifying 'stuff' that makes the world into a meaningful complex world. This process happens under the effect of destabilizing forces of deterritorialization operating within any articulated stratification. As in *Anti-Oedipus*, 'deterritorialization' is here a semiotic concept: society produces surfaces of sense between its stratifications. Deterritorialization is the genetic cause of this production of sense. It is a process of translation between different strata and layers of culture, society and mental activity. It consists of *abstracting ordering principles* from their embodiment within a stratum or a process in order to assign to these ordering principles a more abstract, cultural or even purely cognitive function.

Surfaces of sense are produced by various long-term processes but once they have entered social reality they do not disappear unless they are in turn deterritorialized or pushed aside by competing categories or significations. Thus, any stratification, and any assemblage within socio-historic reality, will be permeated by sense, by bits of category, codification, in short, *sayables* and *thinkables*. These sayables and thinkables are available for members of society to put into words, apply to their own actions or apply to their future actions as a point of orientation.

When we think, it is thus usually by connecting socially available thinkables according to a machine of pragmatic appropriation which is itself assembled according to pre-defined ordering principles: I organize these thinkables into an anecdote, an insult, a road map. It is only through a process of abstraction that thought is able to move beyond the pragmatic appropriation of preconceived thinkables, and move towards thinking the differences between strata and their genetic principles. When thought enters this development it moves in the direction of the diagram, which has as its object the abstract machine. The abstract machine is a composition of determining forces arising from various stratifications, their interactions and the deterritorialized surfaces of senses that exist between them.

Cutting across the determining movement from multiplicity via stratification, deterritorialization to the abstract machine is a more radical form of deterritorialization called the 'line of flight'. Not every deterritorialization is a line of flight, since a deterritorialization simply is the detachment of code from its embodiment, but if deterritorialization affects the function of a stratification, this stratification is sidetracked from its normal mode of operation and enters a different development. The line of flight is the most radical expression of immanence within a social system as it embodies a destabilizing force that affects it from the inside. The lines of flight are indeterminate both with regard to what caused them and in terms of the processes they give rise to. They are lines precisely because they do not have a fixed beginning, middle or end, and like lines they are continuous. They are *lines of flight*, because the change they may produce within the stratification is the only possible change there can be, since no change can ever begin in a subject of choice. For selfhood is itself a rigid stratification, as we shall see in the next section.

Genealogy of the Social Self

Social life is thus organized as a series of overlapping types of organization and deterritorialized surfaces of sense. A social and perceiving, historical and linguistic subject is constructed within this network of intersecting strata and surfaces of sense.

This subject is, like the Oedipal subject in *Anti-Oedipus*, unaware of its own origin. In *A Thousand Plateaus*, the genetic account is considerably more complex, however, and so the differences between how this subject may appear to itself and its actual genesis are both larger and more manifold, as the subject is articulated semiotically along different axes of composition. It is first composed on the level

of the assemblage, as a subject of speech, as an I. Second it is constituted within a trans-historic 'regime of sense', as a depository of
meaning, as a self, or me, that can be referred to by others, and to
which various kinds or meaning, psychological, moral, religious,
etc. can be ascribed. Third, it is circumscribed by molar categories,
that is, binary social categories of gender, wealth, region, etc. that
assign a set of rigid social determinations to it. The subject is thereby
determined as a definite individual, or a 'he' at the intersection of
these determinations.

These axes of constitution are of a very different nature. The
assemblage is located in space and time, it is dynamic and specific.
The trans-historic regime of sense is, on the contrary, extended over
cultural and historical space and time, intertwined and composed
with other such regimes of sense. This historical part of the analysis
is genealogical. It examines the past with a view to understanding
the present and understanding the present differently from how the
present understands itself. Genealogy thus proposes a different
origin for ideal concepts from the origin stipulated within the
society where they are used. A given semiotic regime contains
moral, social, epistemological terms and norms which have a specific social and historical origin but which are reused within new,
composite regimes in which this origin is not known. Finally, the
molar assignment of identity is rigid and static.

There is no thing or substance that would correspond to these
three axes of determination, or that would account for their mode
of composition and coordination. But this open-ended, heteroge-
nous mode of composition is precisely the nature of social and
semiotic processes. They compose with one another in specific and
complex ways that cannot be mapped according to a general model
of society such as, for instance, the structure of class relations in
Marxist social theory. Let us now look more closely at these three
determinations of the social self.

The construction of a subject of speech takes place in language,
but language functions as an anonymous *semiotic machine*, assigning
meanings, syntactical rules, and a particular mode of addressing
reality to individual speakers before they begin to speak. Due to
this prior organization of the language machine before the individual utters a sentence, the utterance itself is collective rather than
individual. It is I who speak, we may say, but Deleuze and Guattari
add: The use of the first person pronoun 'I' always depends on a
prior assemblage of power which gives it forcefulness: I argue, I love
you, I feel, I think. In each case the use of the I function is part of

an assemblage which constitutes the speaker as a subject of power within language. The I is thus the mark of a socially instituted *speech-power.*

Speech itself is always inhabited by other voices. The most basic unit of language is therefore not the word or the sentence but the implicit quotation known as free indirect speech. We never know to what extent we are echoing the thoughts of others and to what extent we are speaking in our own voice. This makes of the act of speaking a social function. We may inhabit this social function in more or less authoritarian ways, confirming or weakening the hold of molar categories of moral or social distinctions on the concrete molecular interaction within which we speak.

Language is molar both in its formal properties of syntax (noun vs verb, present tense vs past tense) and in the division between different pragmatic registers of language use (truthful description vs fictional story, public dispute vs private banter). Due to its molar organization of syntax and pragmatic register, language is a vehicle of power before it becomes a means of communication.

The pragmatic theory of speech-power accounts for how language works as a *machine* operating on already established sayables. This account is now supplemented by an account of how language acquires a content, how specific organized clusters of culturally significant categories are composed. Within the genealogical history of semiotic regimes the cultural categories of selfhood are presented as composites of socially constructed significations without any intrinsic origin. Through the composition of signifying regimes, evolving over time, a 'me' is created. The 'me' functions as a criterion of truth, and a source of meaning in various contexts. The semiotic construct 'me' is then available to speakers of a culture who can apply it to themselves and to others.

The concept of a 'semiotic regime' designates a socially and historically produced level of sense, containing types of things that may be said, or sayables, and assigns to them a social criterion of truth and meaning. The regime has the function of regulating the relationship between the 'I' in the assemblages of speech-power and the social reality in which language operates. It does so by creating divisions which are at once *spatial, social* and *semiotic.*

The basic semiotic principle of the regime is that signs are not universally or homogeneously meaningful and intelligible. For signs presuppose a specific type of intelligibility which is given by the semiotic regime. Regimes are historically specific – but at the same time regimes can outlast their actual existence and become part of other regimes. In modernity, thoughts and categories almost never have their origin in a simple regime but arise out of a crossing of many, historically heterogeneous regimes. The regime is a sphere divided into concentric circles. The smallest circle is the centre of intelligibility within a given social formation, the larger circles those in which signs carry less significance. These circles are all tied to a particular location. Thought then becomes socially governed as a selection and combination of signs from these different spheres. Social divisions do not constitute a fixed system within the regime. They are, rather, threshold values determining a given type of signification: The social rules of signification do not define simply what is permitted and what is not, but characterize different degrees of openness and rigidity of signification. Any society will know characters who are better at connecting different areas of that social world to their own advantage than others. As a system, any set of circles presupposes that it is possible to go far in these connections, that it is possible to make connections that do not conform to the dominant degree of order within that society. If this were not possible, the signifying regime would be closed and become sterile.

With this subtle theory of socio-semiotic circulation of signification Deleuze and Guattari propose *a morphology of the physical and social configurations* which have conditioned the production of signs throughout history. A regime posits relations between signifying practices (preaching, wooing, legislating), social divisions (home, street, castle), types of signs (speech, writing, gesture), and some destabilizing figures (shaman, trader, writer). At the origin of these signifying regimes is religion with its principles of interpretation, its dependence on political power, its spatial divisions and its designation of distinct social-semiotic spheres where signs may circulate in determinate ways. A complete regime of signs can look as follows:

> The complete system, then, consists of the paranoid face or body of the despot-god in the signifying centre of the temple; the interpreting priests who continually recharge the signified in the temple, transforming it into signifier; the hysterical crowd of people outside, clumped in tight circles, who jump from one circle to another; the faceless, depressive scape-goat emanating from the centre, chosen, betrayed, and adorned by the priests, cutting across the circles in his headlong flight into the desert.[8]

Regimes combine in multiple ways, thereby engendering all the
categories of what may be thought of as meaningful, all the primary
categories of social life. A regime is always both political and cultural, made of social relations, forms of power and categories of
intelligibility. Subjectivity itself, as a complex source of intelligibility and criterion of signification, emerges from an intersection
between different regimes. The subject emerges from the intersection of semiotic regimes as a designated source of intelligibility: me
and my feelings, the moral truth of a person, faith, experience, reli-
ability and all the other categories that may be used by a society to
refer to persons and their inner life in order to give substance to
various kinds of judgements about them. It is thus only through the
historical sedimentation and combination of regimes that we have
become moral, legal, religious, psychological subjects. We can then
refer to ourselves and to each other as constituting a particularly
strong concentration of signification.

Through the regime and the assemblage of speech-power, a social
self is constructed. Now this self also exists within social space as
an individual with a definite social and moral identity. In *Anti-
Oedipus*, the formation of a social self presupposed that the psyche
could attribute clear marks of social identity to itself (third paralogism). In *A Thousand Plateaus*, these marks of identity are forms of
social organization by which society is divided by broad 'molar'
categories possessing a rigid binary form: man and woman in the
category of gender; rich and poor in the category of wealth; white
and non-white in the category of race; believer and non-believer in
the category of faith; citizens and non-citizens in the category of
political status. These divisions are exclusive. In molar organization, the self is identified as either man or woman, either rich or
poor, etc. Molar constitutes the sociological parameters through
which individuals identify themselves and each other within the
social realm.

Opposing this form of organization through categorization,
social reality has a second layer of articulation, called 'molecularity'.
This second layer of organization consists of micro-interactions
between people. It takes place in social spaces that may be shaped
by very specific stratifications and assemblages of power, but, as
such, as interaction, molecularity remains irreducible to any of
these prior conditions of stratification or power. Molecularity is
further able to take place across prior divisions and between existing regimes and stratifications. Yet it is equally possible for the
participants in molecular interaction to seek to reaffirm the hold of

established relations of power and semiotic categories within that particular field of interaction.

Molecularity is thereby a site of ambivalence, a site where processes may develop either in the direction of a strengthened molar organization of social relations or in the sense of a line of flight. The molecular is not identical with the line of flight, but the line of flight can only take hold within molecularity. The social subject thus always exists in a force field between molar determinations and molecular potentials for lines of flight. The issue of freedom and responsibility emerges in this tension between molarity and molecularity, a tension that is also played out on the scene of language, in so far as language can also be either molarized, if one affirms its pragmatic registers and syntactic rules or it can be molecularized, used within a smaller context than that of the whole community of language users, thereby withdrawing parts of language from transparent communication. The political problem of fascism also resurfaces in this context. For the fascist state is a state which is not only totalitarian but also in which molar categories have fully absorbed molecular interaction, thus evening out the double articulation.

Since the notions of responsibility and choice are social categories given either through a regime of selfhood (responsibility) or through the enactment of an assemblage (choice), a freedom that does not simply reassert the hold that the socio-semiotic system has over one, cannot itself be expressed as conscious choice. It is tempting for Deleuze and Guattari to define freedom in radical opposition to that of a choice rooted in a socially constituted, stratified subject. This leads to an equation between freedom and a process of destruction of the socially stratified subject. This destructive, radically anti-humanist conception of freedom is also in continuity with the cosmology of Deleuze's early thought. The idea that we ought to reach a sort of union with inanimate matter or the cosmic forces of production before they have become shaped by human beings and interpreted by society pervades all his work. In *A Thousand Plateaus*, it finds expression in the notion of 'tracing a plane of consistency' which means to build up relations outside of any given system of stratification.

The three paradigmatic examples of such a plane of consistency are manifest in religion, sex and certain experiences induced by narcotic drugs. Since religion does not exist outside complex and hierarchical social stratifications and drug consumption produces a rigidly measured and impoverished life, centred as they say on the dealer and the next dose, what remains as a promise of escape is sexuality. They therefore discuss a *Taoist* theory of sexuality which, following Taoism's own principles of immanence, seems to correspond well with the programme of *A Thousand Plateaus*, and thus to be able to suggest a viable escape from selfhood. However, it is not clear that such a practice would be available to a non-Taoist in the right way, that is, available beyond a merely representational appropriation in the categories of 'exoticism' or 'fashion'.

More generally, any attempt at escaping from selfhood, whether induced in the expedient way of narcotic drugs or constructed more laboriously through a particular physical or spiritual exercise, runs the risk of reproducing what it seeks to escape in the form of authoritarian social structures or narcissistic psychological structures.

Immanence and the freedom of immanence, that is the freedom that consists in not applying pre-defined criteria to one's actions and not blocking the movement of desire or creativity with a transcendent judgement, are not attained easily and there is no recipe or technique that can take one there. There are examples of immanence. The Kafka machine exemplified an immanence of writing. Spinoza's philosophy exemplifies for Deleuze a movement of immanence on the plane of thought in that it has systematically eradicated the functions of judgement and transcendence from all their usual strongholds in theology, psychology and moral philosophy. Since even our modes of perceiving and acting – generally speaking, any appropriation of the environment – are pre-structured through the codes of appropriation that we take over from others, to be free cannot mean anything other than to appropriate differently, to select and organize intake from the environment in a non-prescribed and unrepresentable way.

Immanent Freedom: Becoming

Just as the 'nomad', as we saw, is both outside and inside the state, so freedom emerges within systems of social and cognitive organization, but at the same time constitutes a move away from these principles of organization.

This immanence of freedom within order constitutes a break with the implicit Romanticism of *Anti-Oedipus* with its duality of the nomadic subject and the Oedipal subject. In the evolution of Deleuze and Guattari's thought, this erosion of the duality is made possible by the development of the concept of the *machine* in *Kafka: Toward a Minor Literature*. As the Kafka book was written between

Anti-Oedipus and *A Thousand Plateaus*, it constitutes a point of transition where the materialist psychoanalysis of *Anti-Oedipus* is transformed into a general semiotic theory of speech, power and freedom. At this intermediary stage, the machine indicates an engagement with the world and an alternative to the concept of the subject which is richer and more complex than the theory of unconscious desire in *Anti-Oedipus*. The machine marks the transition from desire to action. In *A Thousand Plateaus*, the conceptual role of the machine is taken over by the concept of the assemblage, as a correlation between power and speech, whereas the concept of a desiring subject or an alternative, nomadic subject is replaced by a theory of the 'line of flight' and the 'becoming'.

A line of flight is an unpredictable development that has the formal ontological status of a deterritorialization. Deterritorializations can affect either a whole group or one individual in a group. Likewise, the line of flight is a deterritorialization which affects a group and one or some individuals in the group. It begins on a molecular level of interaction or inter-strata symbiosis – as in the case of parasitic plants – but over time, it can change completely the configuration and functioning of an individual or a group. When the line of flight transforms the stratification of one or several individuals within language and within molar categories, this is called a process of becoming.

As a becoming originates in a line of flight, it further cannot be represented as the outcome of a choice. Becoming therefore constitutes a freedom which does not entail any instance of conscious choice.

A becoming is a very general type of process. It is a composition of activity and passivity, such that it is undecidable what a person does and what simply happens to that person. It is a process that integrates into itself the parameters by which it makes sense and becomes meaningful. As a line of flight, the becoming further cannot be represented subjectively: the becoming is a movement and the question for the individual is whether to continue or to interrupt it, but if it tries to frame and to represent this movement of becoming within a set of moral categories or to evaluate its usefulness, it has already stepped outside the immanent movement of becoming.

The term 'becoming' is also part of a critique of Plato that runs through *A Thousand Plateaus*. In Plato, the concept of 'becoming' (French: *devenir*) means to be in a state of change. This is the property of sensibles and multiples, i.e. the components of the world perceivable through the senses. This realm of becoming is, for Plato, opposed to that which is, and cannot therefore be an object of knowledge. Now becoming in *A Thousand Plateaus* is similarly unknowable. It is thereby protected from molarization: collective utterances made within dominant assemblages of speech-power are not quite able to grasp and to judge a becoming since a becoming is not easily represented within an already existing grid of social and moral coordinates.

Becoming is therefore immanence realized as practice. A becoming occurs in a site where many stratifications interact. It is a *direction* within these intersections, but a direction which is not fully controlled, either consciously or unconsciously by the person. The line of flight as becoming does not possess the kind of underlying intelligence that other thinkers such as Sartre or Freud have ascribed to human behaviour as an unconscious or semi-conscious goal-directedness. Immanence here has a radical meaning, incompatible with the notion of purposefulness. An activity is fully immanent only when it is impossible to see it as purposeful, since it defies the social or communal space in which purposes are judged worthy of pursuit, and pursuits in turn are judged to be true to these purposes.

For becoming is, like the in-between space from which it arises, not located within categorial divisions. Deleuze and Guattari suggest that in the spaces between strata there are loopholes that allow persons or groups to develop in ways which are not fully determined by the antecedent state of that person or group.

Becoming designates for any individual a process of alteration that changes that individual's most basic relations to the world and to itself. This alteration has to be characterized in temporal, semiotic and cognitive terms.

In temporal and causal terms, becomings differ from normal events and actions by being gradual and by being unpredictable. What thus gradually changes are not external determinates of a person, but that person himself. The change is not due to the person taking on a new profession or falling in love or suffering from grief, although such events can trigger a further process of change that may develop into a becoming. Since a becoming is fundamentally unpredictable because it does not flow from an antecedent state, it does not fall within conventional categories of change. The change that a person undergoes in becoming can perhaps best be characterized as a process of *absorption*. A person is absorbed in an activity or in a situation and this increasing absorption changes him or her. To determine further in which respects the person is altered we have to characterize becomings in semiotic and cognitive terms.

What changes in becoming are the person's priorities, categories of classification and general sense of his or her place in the world. A becoming is like a cognitive drift or journey.

Becoming composes elements of its environment in a unique and specific way. It is an articulation of the line of flight as an appropriative desire. Becoming defines immanence as an infra-symbolic realm in which not only parts of the physical environment but also the social and symbolic world surrounding it can be transformed into a component of its development without being mediated through a representation. Thus, becoming realizes the programme of *Anti-Oedipus* of desire as forming an immediate, non-representational relation to social reality. For becoming relates directly to bits of thought and social reality, in the manner of a selector, or a sampling machine, decomposing in order to recompose, indifferent to the category distinction between physical and mental properties, and operating directly on heterogeneous strata.

To become is often to reorganize behaviour and cognition in relation to a molar line of difference, by gradually moving towards a limit of gender or biological species. This movement is different from a conscious imitation and it is different from a transgression: the limit remains an unconscious norm internal to becoming, defining a zone of indetermination. Within this zone of indeterminacy, becoming performs a sampling of traits from the other side of the line and appropriates these traits within its own activity – which becomes reconfigured as a consequence.

The paradigmatic example in *A Thousand Plateaus* of such an appropriative sampling is that of becoming-animal. This becoming is clearly different from a transgression, such as, for instance, cannibalism, for it implies a much more subtle and gradual process of retraining the body and its behaviour.

Thus, in becoming, the body's selections of movements in relation to the environment and of connections with specific parts of the environment take on a new course, guided by a new logic which is defined within and by this process of becoming. Becoming is thereby a process of making oneself select and be affected by forces and parts of the environment that one would normally exclude.

Knowledge and the Abstract Machine

Whenever one analyses an event or a process, one has to uncover its genetic principle within a series of interrelated stratifications. A specific set of stratifications is determined and individuated by the coordination of formal principles which they call an *abstract machine*. To map this abstract machine is to conceive of the genetic principle governing a field of processes.

The aim of science is to produce *diagrams* that capture the functioning of abstract machines. A science can only account for a given level of stratification if it conceives adequately of the level at which different series of stratifications come to function together in specific but indeterminate ways. Science, therefore, has to identify abstract machines enveloping a certain degree of *indetermination*.

One can envisage various applications of this genetic or diagrammatic programme, but if we stay within the field of social reality, we can briefly consider a few candidates for a diagrammatic social theory. In the discipline of history, the diagrammatic method would reinforce a principle which historians, no doubt, already adhere to, namely that the micro-level of human interaction must be related to a heterogeneous field of social inscriptions (ideas, cultural practices) and macro-level transformations of economic and social structure, but the diagrammatic historian would further seek to avoid imposing a determinate structure on these multiple stratifications. In searching for the abstract machine, she would have to take particular care not to choose the object that is to be accounted for within experience, thereby falsely assuming a mirror relation between the actual individuating processes in reality, determined by the abstract machine, and the superficial centres of identity that we encounter in experience. She would thus have to avoid including in the account either as subject matter or as explanatory principles ready-made entities such as an individual life, a political action, a social class or an international conflict.

She could try to achieve this by concentrating on critical points in the spaces of coexistence between systems. She would further be interested in the way that a process simultaneously obeys its own internal logic and yields to external pressures.

The closest one has yet come to a diagrammatic history are probably twentieth-century novelists such as Robert Musil who seek to grasp the relation between events and structures of very different scale and oscillating between surface manifestation and an underlying process of historical transformation. Thus, the remarkable psychological portrait of a mass murderer in Musil's novel *The Man Without Qualities* presents the compulsiveness and texture of a kind of violence which figures as the structural double of the refined and self-absorbed political culture of Austrian elites at the brink of the First World War.

If historians were to follow a similar path, it would not be on the level of narrative, however, but in a formal conception of historical processes as constituted by fragile and complex sets of relations between events and structures of a different kind and order of magnitude.

Another field of diagrammatic social description could be the type of cultural sociology known as cultural theory. The dominant paradigm within contemporary cultural theory is one that combines Hegel and Freud to form a map of social behaviour and signifying practices which makes them intelligible against a historical or political background, as symptoms of the contractions that a society is unable to master.

These dialectical concepts of contradiction have the power to grasp very different kinds of cultural phenomena but at the price of reducing complex constellations of relationships to *dual* relationships of the type *depth–surface, conscious–unconscious, the imaginary–the real*. This perspective is geared towards highlighting a dimension of ideology and anxiety within social reality and cultural practices. It is less able to capture the genetic process through which a specific set of relations is engendered. The diagrammatic method, by contrast, is not a critique of ideology or a diagnosis of contradictions. It is a genetic analysis of how forces of different types come to inhabit the same field of stratification and of the sorts of events and processes which take place between the subsystems of this field. Diagrammatic analysis thus always begins with the questions 'where?', 'when?' and 'how?'. A diagrammatic analysis does not make any assumptions about the natural units of action, its beginning and end points. It follows interactions through their meandering course. The diagrammatist analyses a particular part of reality as a field of sampling: a study of multifaceted stratifications and their intersecting environments. Let us end this presentation of a possible social science with an imaginary case.

If a Hegelian cultural theorist were to analyse the death of Princess Diana, she might begin by looking at the transformations of the English class system, the way in which the middle class is over-laid by working-class identifications and how it has historically sought to assert itself vis-à-vis the aristocracy. Then she might look at the relations between the signifiers embodied by Diana, sport–sexuality–youth–charity–ordinariness against the background of this fragility of the middle class. She would analyse whether the worship of Diana might reveal a significant pattern of wish fulfilment and masked anxiety.

The diagrammatic analyst would follow a very different path. She would begin by looking at the network of paparazzi and the circuits of finance that Diana was involved in at the moment of her death. Then she might investigate the ambivalent becoming-visible of Diana. Was her strange relationship with the camera perhaps always a form of self-effacement? Then the diagrammatist would analyse the relationship between sexuality, power, gender, animals and materials such as clothes and food in the royal family and the Spencer household.

Thus, whereas the Freudo-Hegelian analyst traces *dominant identifications and anxieties*, the diagrammatist establishes networks between *power, sexuality, ideas* and *cultural productions* without any pre-established hierarchy between these different stratifications.

Power, Thought, Action

Now we may ask: what is Deleuze and Guattari's project in *A Thousand Plateaus*? Are they attempting to *save* the reader? Are they producing a theory of social production and signifying practice? Are they reflecting on the nature of rationality or constructing the base for a critique of power?

They are performing all of these tasks, but the difficulty of *A Thousand Plateaus* stems from the perfect simultaneity of these different actions and intellectual processes. In *A Thousand Plateaus*, the dominant theme – the opposition between authority and attempts to flee the effects of authority – is splintered into different directions by the book's various strands. Authority manifests itself in thought, in our minds as well as in science and micro-activities. To study authority as a thought form is then both to examine how human beings behave individually and in groups, but also to study various systems of signification. The account does not have one starting-point, such as desire, reason, power, the modern state, creativity or life. It migrates from area to area and from stratum to stratum. Thus the appropriative principle of becoming applies to the enterprise of *A Thousand Plateaus* itself. The theoretical programme of *A Thousand Plateaus* is to formulate a completely new conception of our place in the world, of what it is to act, to feel and to think. This conception entails that there is *nothing in us that is not social*, that everything that we do has political and historical implications and that our ordinary ways of representing what we do underestimate the interconnectedness and simultaneity of the processes that we take part in. This new conception also challenges sociological common sense founded on the ontological duality, inherited from political philosophy, between the individual and society.

Social subjects are constructed along the three axes of the assemblage that makes it into a vehicle of collective utterances, the regime that makes it a referent and depository of psychological and moral significations, and the molar categorizations that locate the subject as a well-defined social individual within a grid of social determinations. In the most molarized cases these three subjects coincide. The utterance 'I love you' manifests a subject of speech, refers to a subject of meaning and designates itself as a potential lover with a determinate social identity but the three axes of determination can also come apart or co-exist in an indeterminate way. Deleuze and Guattari often say that the greatest potentials for change and innovation come from the least expected quarters.

Freedom from social determination is enacted through becomings which, as they are lines of flight that cannot be chosen, fall outside of the representational framework of judgement according to values, purposes and other socially recognizable criteria. Freedom is thus essentially a moral freedom from the structure of judgement and the application of criteria, whether this judgement would be located in oneself (moral subject) or in others (collective utterances of values).

There is no conceptual continuity between this subject of becoming and its negative freedom and the moral and social subject that it flees. In other words, there is no discursive or pragmatic arena, an arena of politics or of discussion, where the two kinds of subjectivity could meet or be confronted with one another. The subject of becoming remains at the margins of social stratification.

The formal ontology through which this description is conducted also has further, epistemological implications for how we think about ourselves, about social reality, and about any kind of being – including thought itself. From the point of view of the ontology of stratifications, the normal cognitive operations of representation never appear to conceive of a process or an event in the adequate order of magnitude. It is both too close – overlooking the space between, the environment – and too distant – overlooking the simultaneity of stratifications in each being. Representation therefore cannot articulate the way a process is involved spatially and historically with others. It isolates parts of a process and calls it a thing, a subject, an institution, a cause, but it does not see what constitutes these so-called things, subjects, institutions and causes, materially and semiotically. It does not see that there is always a multiplicity of causal series active in any event (the abstract machine) and that the beings it isolates from their actual and material process of being derive their consistency from the political power that is operative in them and the semiotic principles that they imply.

Representation also resists understanding its own genetic origin within stratification. For representational thought is itself the effect of a complex stratified process, the manifestation of statehood in thought as a centralizing, hierarchical mode of cognition and ordering which seeks to map all of being onto one semiotic plane organized by one set of coordinates. This origin of representation can of course not be articulated within representation itself. There is thus nothing left for representation to think, not even itself. The Cartesian, Kantian and Husserlian philosophy of the subject had as its programme to understand thought from within the space of mental representation, thereby providing an ideal self-understanding of representation. In *A Thousand Plateaus*, this programme is made the object of a very fundamental attack that has yet to be met.

5

Philosophy and Art

The Nature of Philosophy

I shall end this account of Deleuze's thought with a discussion of Deleuze's theory of philosophy, his books on painting and cinema and his study of Leibniz and the baroque, called *The Fold*: *Leibniz and the Baroque* (1988).[1] As we shall see, these three areas of enquiry are closely intertwined in Deleuze's thought. Thus he comes to conceive of philosophy as a practice analogous to art, and to conceptualize art as a creation of thought analogous to philosophy.

Deleuze conceives of philosophy as an *immanent creation*. We have seen that the term 'immanent' has different meanings in his philosophy. Here immanence means that philosophy creates concepts and problems which only exist and gain their content within philosophy. But what, then, is philosophy if it can generate the content of the concepts and problems that define it?

Deleuze's theory of philosophy is presented, first, in his book on Nietzsche and then, a few years later, developed further in *Difference and Repetition* and completed in the work co-written with Guattari: *What Is Philosophy?* This theory conceives of philosophy as a kind of creation or construction. Philosophy is thus not a description or intuition of reality. Philosophy consists in the construction of a plane. On this plane it invents and combines concepts. These concepts are the articulations of problems. Neither the 'concept' nor the 'problem' is external to philosophy; both exist on the immanent plane of philosophy.

The problem is an internal limitation on the invention of concepts. The concept and the problem are related in such a way that a concept only becomes meaningful in relation to a problem. The problem in turn is determined exclusively by and within a network of concepts. Thus concepts and problems define each other. This relationship between concepts and problems serves to demarcate philosophy in relation to 'ordinary thought' arising within everyday experience. In ordinary thought one may express opinions and general intuitions but these intuitions and opinions are too vague and indeterminate to define either a concept or a problem. The distinction between philosophy and opinion is familiar from philosophy and resembles distinctions made, for instance, by Plato between *doxa* and *episteme*, opinion and knowledge. Deleuze does not characterize philosophy as knowledge or the search for truth. He does not characterize philosophical thought by its relation to an outside about which it would purport to produce knowledge. His conception of philosophy is thus radically constructivist: philosophy is a practice of immanent invention which is not answerable to any external instance of truth – such as God, experience or scientific theories.

The question then arises, if philosophy is not regulated by a norm of truth or an ideal of knowledge, what makes *philosophy philosophical*? What do great philosophical texts have in common which makes them different from religious sermons, scientific treatises, or works of art? Deleuze argues that what they have in common is a systematic and radical *immanence*. Whereas science relies on empirical experiments and art refers to sensory experience of some kind, philosophy is in its aspirations at least, independent of this reference to experience and to the world of experience.

The task faced by any philosopher as a result of this radical immanence is to produce a system of concepts and problems that has a sufficient internal consistency and specificity in order not to collapse into mere opinion. Philosophy derives this consistency from the internal *systematicity* of its constructions. This systematicity in turn is not identical with any one particular method – such as Cartesian Analysis of Ideas, Hegelian Dialectic or the Logical Analysis of so-called 'analytical' philosophy. There is not one single method of philosophy, just as there is not one single model of philosophical exposition. This is because the image that philosophy has produced about its own activity has always been transcendent and dogmatic, measuring philosophy against some ideal of truth that it is supposed to attain. Philosophy has, as a consequence, also been dogmatic in its conceptions of what constitutes an appropriate method of thinking. It has sought to devise models of correct reasoning in order to aid the philosophical mind in its pursuit of the ideal truth, but philosophy is not governed by this sound and narrow path of reason.

Philosophical systematicity is different from such a path in that it is governed neither by specific argumentative or rationalistic norms nor by an end point of truth and knowledge. Philosophical systematicity is internal to the philosophical systems that display the quality of systematicity and does thus not answer to any general and external criterion. There is no external judgement and no general criterion which can determine which method of doing philosophy, that of Spinoza or that of Heidegger, for instance, is better, or more systematic.

What characterizes an important philosophical system is that it invents new problems which it spells out and articulates with the aid of its own concepts. Often these concepts are taken from the tradition, but they are then given a new meaning through the process of articulating a new problem. Let us take as an example Spinoza's use of conventional Aristotelian concepts to articulate a new set of problems.

Spinoza identifies a problem of immanence. As soon as this problem is articulated in philosophy, it gives rise to new subsidiary problems. In defining the relation between God and the world as a relationship of immanent creation, Spinoza produces problems about how the finite created being relates to the divine being that produced it, of how, more specifically, the finite being is different from, yet in some sense identical to, infinite divine nature, of how the finite can belong within infinite nature.

These particular problems are articulated within the system through the concepts of 'substance', 'mode', 'attribute' and 'cause': the finite mode is internal to divine substance; substance is a cause of itself and modes have their cause of existence outside of themselves, in substance. The attribute is a common ground between substance and mode, the route along which the substantial cause expresses itself. The terms substance, mode, attribute and cause belong to the Aristotelian tradition of philosophy. In medieval philosophy these terms refer to the being of individual things (substances), their qualities (modes, attributes), and their development (efficient, formal, final causes). In Spinoza's philosophy of immanence these concepts are redefined as they are employed in the articulation of a new problem.

Deleuze's theory of concepts, problems and immanent creation bears a strong resemblance to the theory of science developed in France by Gaston Bachelard, Georges Canguilhem and Michel Foucault. While Deleuze was never a historian of science, he took a vivid interest in the work of Michel Foucault, particularly in his theory of speech and history, the *Archaeology of Knowledge*. Deleuze wrote a very positive review of this book when it came out. This text appears in a revised version in the book that Deleuze published on Foucault after his death. Deleuze's reading of the *Archaeology of Knowledge* brings to light a normative problem in Foucault's method which is of relevance also for his own theory of philosophy: the border between what belongs to knowledge and what does not, *is itself part of knowledge* and *cannot, therefore, be derived from experience*. In Deleuze's theory of philosophy, concepts are therefore rigorously defined by their relations to other concepts – they are neither derived from experience, nor are they to be conceived as tools which we can use to describe experience – or reality in a wider sense. Concepts are constructs forming a reality of their own. They also exist in a different way from sentences or ideas. Concepts do not form part of language or the mind. In *What Is Philosophy?*, Deleuze and Guattari sketch what they call the environment of concepts. The concept exists on a 'plane' surrounded by other concepts. The plane is itself internal to philosophy. Philosophy creates the medium (plane) in which it invents concepts.

The notion of a plane raises a difficult question about philosophical immanence: is philosophy immanent also in the sense of being without presuppositions? Does not thinking always begin by implying a range of tacit assumptions? In *What Is Philosophy?*, Deleuze and Guattari address this problem. In distinguishing immanence of construction from the ideal immanence of a completely self-sufficient and self-justifying rational system, in the manner in which, for instance, Hegel understood such a system, they seek to reconcile the idea of immanent construction with the notion that this constructive practice may well have porous borders: the plane is thus different from a rational space of enquiry or an ideal realm of eternal forms. Philosophical practice does not take place in a historical, cultural and political vacuum. Nor is philosophical practice reducible to any external conditions. Philosophical practice, in absorbing elements of its contemporary surroundings, transforms them into its own set of presuppositions. So, rather than having external conditions, philosophy invents its own conditions. These conditions define, prior to any problem or concept, a minimal sense of what it means to be real. Thus, prior to the philosophical concept of 'Being' and the problems attached to this concept, philosophy will at any given time make assumptions about what it means to count as real. This tacit and pre-conceptual assumption then permeates the plane of philosophical creation. We may take as an example the three problems addressed by each of Kant's three 'critiques': what guarantees the validity of empirical judgements? What justifies moral action? What is the ground of aesthetic judgements? These problems are coordinated and gain consistency as forming one cluster of distinct and yet related problems because Kant implicitly and tacitly makes a primary assumption about norms and judgements: he conceives of ideal norms of validity and legitimacy as having an unquestionable force in the world, irreducible to any physical or natural force.

The immanent plane is therefore like a threshold value of initial assumptions which cannot be questioned within that philosophy and without which that philosophy would not be able to construct concepts and identify problems. The old logical term 'petition of principle' indicates the circularity that an argument produces when it implicitly uses a principle that it sets out to prove. This kind of circularity is, Deleuze would argue, a necessary condition of philosophy. It is only within a set of assumed, but not fully articulated, principles about reality that there can be construction of concepts in relation to determinate problems. This means that we should not expect of philosophical arguments that they are absolutely clear or transparent as the dogmatic norms of rationality would seem to require. The practice of philosophy is always tied to implicit, unconscious assumptions that guide it and the aim of clarity cannot apply to these implicit assumptions themselves. The philosophical ideal of total self-understanding is thus an illusion stemming from a misinterpretation of the creative autonomy that philosophy enjoys as conceptual invention.

This definition of philosophical practice as conceptual creation corresponds to Deleuze's own philosophical self-understanding as a systematic empiricist. Empiricism means for Deleuze a rejection of any metaphysical justification of reality. Philosophy thus proceeds without ever reaching an absolute truth but it does produce systematic relations between concepts. Deleuze and Guattari extend this conception of philosophy to the whole history of philosophy with Plato and Descartes as its central figures: if the purest rationalists can be framed within this constructivist non-metaphysical view of philosophical practice, philosophy as an activity is not dependent on the 'dogmatic image of thought', the definition of philosophy as a rational enquiry and a metaphysical description of reality. This constructivism brings philosophy close to *art*. The last period of Deleuze's work is therefore devoted to a series of texts in which he compares philosophy and art.

Philosophy and Art

For Deleuze, thought is not closed around itself as a mental realm. Thought exists equally in artistic practices, in institutions, in scientific theories. Thought can be defined independently of psychology if the logic of sense constitutes the *logical inside* of thought, not as it appears in introspection, but the inside of thought as it emerges from its own internal, structural possibilities.

This structural inside can be expressed in various practices, in science, in art or in philosophy. One can think of the whole of Deleuze's later work as an effort to define a logic of thought that would be embodied in sensory relations. This leads in the books on Leibniz, on Foucault and his books on cinema to a productive interface between philosophy and art. During this period he conceives of art as thought embodied in a sensory medium and sees philosophy as a practice of formal construction analogous to art. Deleuze thereby seeks to define the medium of thought independently of how thought is experienced, by seeing thought as the tracing of relations within an abstract sensory space.

The works on Foucault and Leibniz explore this interface with art from the point of view of philosophy, as an aesthetic configuration of concepts. In his book *The Fold*, Deleuze reconstructs the metaphysical and rationalistic system of Leibniz according to the sensuous and tactile concept of the 'fold' which he finds instantiated, equally, in the structure of Leibniz's ontology and in baroque architecture. In his book on Foucault (1986), he reconstructs the Foucauldian history of knowledge and institutions as being based on a historical a priori principle, which in turn he sees divided between a *form of the sayable* and a *form of the visible*, or as he says, an organization of what can be said correlated with an organization of *light*. In his two-volume work on cinema, *Cinema I* and *II* (1983, 1985), Deleuze compares the organization of sense in film to a cognitive process, and thus equates the greatest films to processes of abstract thought capable of presenting a non-empirical composition of time.

The aesthetic theory of thought pursues the earlier project of a semiotics of sense. The fundamental principle of this aesthetic theory emerges from the transcendental semiotics of sense: anything that we may think or express, anything that we can conceive of as *signifying* or simply *ordered*, is dependent on divisions and ordering principles which may be expressed either in philosophy, as concepts, or in a sensory medium as relations of light and lines. Whereas the semiotic project was primarily concerned with language and thus found its most adequate embodiment in literature, the aesthetics of thought that evolves in Deleuze's thought during the 1980s is concerned with ordering principles outside of language. The interface of philosophy and visual art is thus conducive to a more radical problematization of representation. For if philosophy is like a visual work of art, thought does not primarily consist of representing reality but in creating configurations upon an abstract plane of expression. The immanence of thought is thus what is at stake here. In order for the exercise of philosophy to be conceivable as an immanent discipline, the conventional tie between thought and representation has to be severed. The interface with art shows how this is possible. Let us now consider how this problem is carried out in the book on Leibniz and baroque art, *The Fold*.

The Fold defines a minimal structural element of thought that is both conceptual and sensual. The 'fold' is a historically specific thought, or thought form, the thought that animates architecture, mathematics, biology, logic and philosophy in a certain strand of late seventeenth-century European culture called the baroque. The fold is manifest in the robes of statues, in the organization of light and shadow in churches, in the mathematics of curbs and cones, in Leibniz's philosophy of nature and subjectivity.

Leibniz understands all being as existing in continuity with everything else. At the same time all that exists is, and is determined as, an individual. The ultimate constituents of reality are individual spirits called *monads*. These spirits are centres of energy expressing themselves as strings of perceptions. In the case of human beings some of these perceptions become self-conscious thought. The two ontological principles, the individuality of monads and the continuity of being, are reconciled in Leibniz's system because the content of these perceptions is the same. Every perception contains all of the universe, that is all the other monads and their perceptions. The perceptions are nevertheless not absolutely identical. They differ in the way this content is ordered. Likewise, the monads are not completely identical but differ in the sequence of their perceptions and the degree to which they attain self-consciousness. Only in God's mind are all the perceptions that constitute the world present simultaneously. The word 'fold' appears in Leibniz's texts as a means of referring to perceptions that are not self-conscious. The monad is thus said to be like a cloth that is infinitely folded. In the monad only a very small part of this folded cloth is present to self-conscious thought at any given time. Deleuze takes up this term of the fold and extends its use from being a metaphor to being the central thought in Leibniz's system. The fold can be said to define both continuity and individuality – the two polar extremes of Leibniz's philosophy. All being is *continuous* because instead of being divided, nature is itself like an immense folded cloth with infinitely many organisms at different levels of organization and complexity. At the highest level there is the human soul in which individuality is folded as self-consciousness. There is no separation between distinct entities. There are just centres of activity folded within larger centres of activity. The individuality of the human being puts a limit on this folding, because the human soul is the highest form of unity within the created world. All the properties of an individual are inherent in that individual as virtual properties folded within its soul.

Deleuze's reading produces several parallel processes of transformation. It translates what is Platonic in Leibniz into a sensory and non-hierarchical language. Deleuze subordinates both the logic of predication (the monad's properties) and the metaphysics of the monad (the principle of unity) to the sensory logic of the fold. The process of acquiring form through folding becomes the central feature of reality and not the metaphysical unity and identity of the monadic soul or self. *The self is necessary only as the point where the fold is organized.* The reading identifies a particular moment in the argument as its organizing centre in order to recast the whole of Leibniz's philosophy from being a logical and metaphysical system founded upon a theory of truth, to being a conceptual image of reality as a sensory balance between individuality and continuity. Deleuze does not criticize Leibniz. He constructs his own philosophy within Leibniz's philosophy.

We have seen that Deleuze has the critical project of showing the inadequacy of the Aristotelian subject-predicate logical form as a building block in philosophy. Leibniz, however, appears to use exactly this model when he says that the monads are primary substances and that the string of perceptions that make up the inner life of the monad are its predicates, contained within its 'complete notion'. In order to save the baroque Leibniz from Leibniz the logician, Deleuze elaborates a distinction between two logical concepts, which he terms *inclusion* and *attribution*. If all that happens in the monad's life (its perceptions) can be assimilated to predicates, the reverse is also true: *all predicates can be assimilated to events*. The contents of the complete notion must therefore be seen, not as a set of attributes, but in terms of what it refers to, which is the string of perceptual events included in the monad's life.

The monad's perceptions are unified within its complete notion which is also the appearance of the monad in the divine mind. This metaphysics of divine intelligence foreseeing and ultimately causing every event – since the monads are identical with created being – constitute another challenge for Deleuze's reading. Deleuze's ontology of chance and virtual composition is not compatible with a conception of the world as a deterministic system controlled by a divine intelligence. However, Deleuze now argues that Leibniz's theology of creation, in which God chooses between different possible worlds, entails a baroque complexity: it involves an immense system of combinations from which a choice has to be made, a choice not simply between sets of individuals but between the sets of events that make up these individuals. Challenging the theology of creation in Leibniz's philosophy Deleuze now claims that the being of the monad itself corresponds to this selection process. The monad moves forward through its perceptions by selecting at each instance from its infinite storage those that will be composed into conscious experience. Deleuze thus, by emphasizing the selection process, shifts the focus from the divine intellect to the finite being of the monad, conceiving of the selection process as the event by which the universe as an open-ended process moves forward.

Following this interpretation of the monad as a fluid plastic form, the other tenets of Leibniz's philosophy will also be interpreted as sensory processes rather than logical structures. Deleuze establishes an analogy between baroque art and Leibniz's monadology based on the separation between outside and inside, façade and interior. Baroque architecture organizes light so as to display a vivid contrast with darkness. Light contrasts with and thereby serves to emphasize closure, producing inside the closed space a local and circumscribed luminosity. A similar structure characterizes the monad. Without windows, as Leibniz says, it cannot interact with anything outside it. Inside its closed order of perceptions, a few perceptions are at any point in time highlighted as they pass before the eye of the mind and become self-conscious thought. The relationship between light and darkness in baroque art is not only one of contrast but also of degrees. The *chiaroscuro* technique of Caravaggio or Rembrandt aims to paint the gradual emergence of form against the background of increasing darkness and indifferentiation. The same holds true of our ordinary thoughts in Leibniz's monadology. They slide before us, partly illuminated in self-consciousness but quickly become absorbed into the darkness of our unconscious perceptions. Which perceptions are at the centre of attention and which are plunged into darkness constantly changes as the mind is propelled forward through the course of its life:

> The chiar-oscuro fills the monad according to a series which one can go through in both directions: at one end the dark background, at the other end the sharp light, which when it lights up produces whiteness in the designated area, but the white darkens more and more, is replaced by obscurity, an ever thicker shadow as it spreads towards the dark corners in all of the monad.[2]

Let us now consider how the parallel works the other way, how, that is, art may resemble philosophy.

Cinema and the Critique of Representation

Deleuze's two-volume work on cinema, *L'image-mouvement* and *L'image-temps*, translated as *The Movement-Image* and *The Time-Image*, presents cinema as a conflictual field of thought, an arena where two fundamentally different ways of organizing thought and creating relations clash. One is representational and based on narrative conventions; the other, the cinema of modernity, challenges the conventions of narrative cinema and thereby challenges representation itself. Narrative cinema constitutes a 'movement-image'. Cinematic modernity has opposed to the movement-image a different way of organizing the image and of organizing the relationship between the image and time, the 'time-image'.

Deleuze is unique among philosophers of the late twentieth century in having written systematically on cinema. Deleuze is not what we now call a 'film theorist', nor is he a film critic. He neither taught film nor did he write film reviews. He watched films and he thought about them, in the light of theoretical debates on cinema in France, often originating in the journal *Cahiers du Cinéma*. French film historians and critics developed a problem of cinematic modernity defined around the concept of *mise en scène*, the narrative organization of the visual image. Deleuze produces a philosophical interpretation of *mise en scène* within the context of an opposition, inherited from this French critical tradition, between narrative realism and cinematic modernity.

A more intrinsic definition of Deleuze's work on cinema is that it attempts to articulate an aesthetics of film from the point of view of the film itself in abstraction from the conditions of film production and film reception. Film is for Deleuze above all an aesthetic medium. He does not therefore accept the assumption shared by some film theorists that film is a means of *communication*. Film is an immanent field of sense, organizing affects and time into an autonomous whole which is neither representational nor defined by its relations to a film audience. Film is thus for Deleuze neither to be analysed as a representation of a reality outside the film nor as a means to create an impact on an audience.

Film is, rather, a cognitive art form. It organizes visual elements in time. Thereby it performs a mind-like operation. The organization of the film image stands in a complex relation to ordinary cognition and perception. It cannot be derived from ordinary experience: the laws of composition and editing are not identical to the patterns of perception and cognition in subjective experience. On the other hand, a film can, to a higher or a lesser degree, seek to be faithful to the way elements are organized in ordinary subjective experience. This means that some films can challenge the order that we impose on the world within ordinary experience whereas others endorse this representational order.

The focus of his analysis is always on the composition of individual frames and their relations to one another in editing. The aim of the analysis is to understand the cognitive achievements of different film-makers and types of film. The visual qualities of the film image and the cognitive implications of these qualities are then conceived as autonomous, immanent features of the film. This theory of intrinsic qualities resembles a method of *semiotics*, but it has an ambiguous relation to conventional semiotic film theory which aims to quantify the narrative units or segments of a film. Against this narrative semiotics Deleuze develops a *qualitative* semiotic of cinema, a theory of how aesthetic and signifying qualities of the film image are organized independently of the narrative units into which the film may be divided such as scenes or sequences.

Deleuze aims to present the film image as an autonomous signifying reality, as a kind of signification that in no way is derived from a representation of the world. In the history of cinema, such an autonomous image had to liberate itself slowly from a type of film that is organized around characters and the telling of stories. This narrative cinema has constituted the mainstream of film-making both in Hollywood and elsewhere.

There are two overlapping divisions in the cinema books geared towards grasping this distinction between narrative and non-narrative cinema. The first, which occupies a central place in the argument of the first volume, *The Movement-Image*, is between showing the world in pragmatic and human terms, and showing the material world and the human body outside of any reference to action. This distinction points to a way in which any narrative film can develop an abstract image that detaches itself from its own plot and from the reference to the actions and reactions of characters. The second division which defines the border between the first and the second volume, entitled *The Time-Image*, concerns a much more general trend of aesthetic *abstraction*, i.e. of a mode of composition which relies more on the stylistic qualities of the film image than on the narrative content that it represents. This possibility of aesthetic abstraction occurs at different moments within European, American and Japanese cinema but in each case it is seen by Deleuze as an *affirmation of the visual and aesthetic autonomy of the film image*.

According to Deleuze, classical or mainstream narrative cinema is organized around an ideal correspondence between *camera* and *character* so that what the camera frames and films corresponds in principle to what a character within the fiction would be able to see. This correspondence creates an anchoring of the film image within a framework of subjective perception. The artificial gaze of the camera is mediated through the perception and action of characters. The camera is thus not an anonymous or objective or impersonal gaze, but an individual gaze that is presented as a stand-in for the natural perception of the character. This character gaze is further expressed as a pragmatic subject, as a subject of action. According to the conventions of mainstream narrative cinema, it is not enough for the characters to occupy a position in the film frame, they also have to respond actively to a pragmatic situation, i.e. they have to *act*. The world viewed by the camera-character is thus always a world that is present to an active subject, it is always a world *that is about to be acted upon*.

The move beyond classical narrative was accomplished by what is conventionally called 'modern cinema', the 'art cinema' of, for instance, Ozu or Antonioni. This cinema breaks with the correlation between the visual frame and the perceiving and pragmatic character-subject of the movement-image. In this new cinema the image presents a *disembodied* view on the world. Cinematic modernity thus liberates the film image from an anchoring within a perceiving and acting subject. This new image thereby develops signification within the image directly and not with reference to action. Through this movement of abstraction, cinematic modernity also liberates a potential inherent to film as an art form. This potential concerns the intrinsic relationship between film and time. Film is, according to Deleuze, an *immanent field of signification*, capable of organizing time in a way that is not derived from experience.

At the same time, a film can, to a higher or a lesser degree, be faithful to the way elements are organized in ordinary experience. This, on the other hand, means that *some* films can challenge the representational order of ordinary experience, whereas others, that is, classical narrative cinema, largely conform to the order of perception and subjective experience. The difference between a direct presentation of time in the time-image and a re-presentation of time through a narrative perspective in the movement-image involves the ontological relationship between *time and change*. In the movement-image, time is represented only relative to change and movement. We must here not think of movement in physical terms but, more abstractly, as the alteration that occurs within a narrative situation, the alteration on which narrative is based. Since narrative thus presupposes the notion of a situation which is altered, the movement-image requires a certain kind of dramatic organization of the narrative world in the film and of the image itself. In order to be intelligible as the alteration of a situation, the story needs to contain certain psychological, thematic, spatial and dramatic relationships, those relations namely that make up the situation and its process of change. In the movement-image, the representation of these types of relation has been the defining trait of the development of film style, according to Deleuze.

The visual 'grammar' of narrative cinema, the basic rules of composition for telling a story in images, involves camera position and framing, spatial relations within the frame, editing rhythm, use of sound and dialogue, as well as the organization of the story itself. Given the requirements of narrative just mentioned, the primary principle of this visual grammar in the movement-image is contrast. A differential element is employed to define each part or component of the visual image in relational terms, as meaningful in relation to something else in the image, or in relation to a previous image. This visual grammar of narrative cinema evolved, Deleuze writes, during the 1920s and 1930s. The suspense editing of Griffith, the thematic editing (montage) of Eisenstein, the opposition of light and shadow in German expressionist film-makers like Murnau and Lang, and the contrast between the sea and the mainland in the French film-makers Renoir and Grémillion are basic elements of narrative and visual composition, assuring a structural and visual coherence of meaning within the film. Thereby, the visual field is defined by a set of meaning-bearing relations. To break away from narrative cinema thus implies presenting a visual image that is not defined by its contrastive relations of meaning. The change from the move-ment-image to the time-image thus implies a change in the signify-ing status or quality of the film image itself, a movement away, that is, from meaning-bearing relations.

In narrative cinema, i.e. the movement-image, the film image is primarily a sign or a bearer of narrative and relational meaning and only secondarily a visual image. The time-image turns this around: the visual image is first and foremost a reality in its own right and then, secondarily, a bearer of meaning, but this meaning need not be developed dramatically nor be presented through relations within the image or between images.

One need only compare the way a classical American film-maker such as William Wyler tends to film houses in his melodramatic and suspense-laden narrative cinema to how a house is filmed in a modern European film like Victor Erice's *The Spirit of the Beehive* (1973). In quite different types of films such as *The Little Foxes*, a Southern family melodrama from 1941, or *The Desperate Hours*, a suspense film about escaped prison convicts from 1955, Wyler employs the same dramatic, spatial and contrastive style. He thus excels in exploiting the narrative potential of the house within the story, in both these films a large two-storey house with a prominent staircase: he then effectively uses the borders between rooms, the relation between upstairs and downstairs, the dynamic space of the staircase as dramatic devices to emphasize the suspense and the affective potential of the story. In Erice, by contrast, the house takes on a reality of its own which seems to be equal in weight to that of its inhabitants. The characters in *The Spirit of the Beehive* are pas-sively resisting the Franco regime after the Spanish Civil War, living on a large and slightly desolate country estate. The house and the characters are equal, both have been left out of history, both are waiting for better times. The characters move around in the house but the house does not accentuate their relationships to one another.

This example concerns space rather than time and it is indeed more obvious to think of visual abstraction in spatial rather than temporal terms. Yet Deleuze has a complex argument to explain why abstraction in cinema emerges from a particular presentation of time.

Whereas time in narrative cinema is aligned to a change within a dramatic situation, the time-image renders time *directly*, as a virtual composition within the image itself. The time presented within the time-image is thus not that of a change or of a dramatic development; it is not embedded within conflicts and character relations. Typically this direct presentation of time takes the form of rendering characters as *components* of a space rather than the *centre* of a space. The space will then connote the temporal quality of permanence, or repetition or stasis, which weighs on the characters or relativizes the significance of their actions. The time-image is therefore close to Deleuze's earlier, metaphysical, conception of *destiny* as a repetition and variation of virtualities: the time-image presents different stations of a particular destiny, a particular segment of repetition-variation. This anti-pragmatic conception of time and of life corresponds to some film-makers in particular. In Ozu's films, characters often appear to be dominated by their domestic environment. Visconti presents characters who seem unable to break free of their historical and social situation. Welles invents characters who appear to be trapped within a role that they cannot escape but only repeat. The characters in the films of Alain Resnais are victims of repetition on an even grander scale, as the repetition that controls them seems no longer to be part of a forward-moving time line.

Deleuze's conception of cinematic modernity as implying a break with a pragmatic and humanistic perspective on the world thus also has a strongly conservative or fatalistic dimension: the film-makers who most fully exemplify the time-image are seen by Deleuze in terms of his own fatalistic conception of time. This movement from modernity to fatalism is characteristic of a deeper ambiguity in Deleuze's thought, flowing from his deep-seated critique of any anthropocentric view on the world. Thus, the liberation from representation and humanism, which is repeated in various ways throughout his books, constitutes a move towards an affirmation of fate.

Art, Ethics and Subjectivity

In his book on the painter Francis Bacon, *Francis Bacon: The Logic of Sensation* (1981), Deleuze develops a different moral theme from that of the fatality embodied in the time-image. The book presents the notion of a subject that is located outside any representational order. This theme was announced in *A Thousand Plateaus* through the theory of *becoming*, presenting an ethical potential defined in opposition to representation. Becoming contains a minimal subject that is also defined in opposition to the socially defined moral subject. The issue of subjectivity that is addressed in the book on Francis Bacon, written during the same period as *A Thousand Plateaus*, thus concerns both representation, as a thought form, and the ethics of an a-representational subject.

A Thousand Plateaus argues that the morally accountable subject, formed through a constellation of the 'I' of speech-power, the 'me' of moral responsibility, and the 'he' or 'she' that falls within large social and moral categories, is the product of a highly complex, historical and semiotic, process. The book also argues that a very different kind of subject, a subject of *becoming* can emerge at the margins of these processes. The subject of becoming is a-representational. It is neither a subject taking up a position within discourse, nor a subject that is representable according to existing parameters of purposeful action. What is, we may ask, the relationship between the subject of becoming and 'freedom'? The theory of 'becoming' entails a notion of freedom as *escape* and a parallel notion of *creation* emerging from this movement of escape. In so far as this freedom-in-creation exists, it is a-representational. It is a freedom emerging within the radical immanence of a self-defining, self-structuring development that sets its own criteria of success or failure as it evolves. This immanent freedom of the subject of becoming is thus in a particular sense unspeakable. It is not hidden or invisible but it does not fall within the domain of any existing discourse.

In his own late works Deleuze addresses these questions of subjectivity, freedom and creation and he does so largely within the domain of *aesthetics*. Deleuze thus makes aesthetics into a sort of master discipline of philosophy, replacing the ontology of sense and repetition from the early work. In the aesthetic texts on art and philosophy from his late work – the texts on Foucault, Leibniz, cinema and Francis Bacon – Deleuze articulates an understanding of subjectivity that is different from the Kantian or Husserlian concepts of consciousness, but also clearly separate from any subject of agency, decision and political or moral responsibility.

In his book on the painter Francis Bacon, Deleuze analyses how modern painting, and the works of Cézanne, Van Gogh and Bacon in particular, treat the problem of pictorial representation. His guiding idea in *Francis Bacon: The Logic of Sensation* is that Bacon strives to purify the representation of the human body by voiding it of all illustrative content. There is an evolution in Bacon's work from dramatic and spectacular pictures to a more sober exploration of the human body framed by geometrical lines. The later paintings isolate the body within the frame, rendering its positions, movements and affects, without the realist coordinates of a social environment filled with objects, people or even human interaction.

Bacon's aesthetic evolves gradually in the course of his work as he purifies the rendering of the body itself, presented as a composition of affects. This development culminates in a series of triptychs from the early 1970s in which the body is framed within large monochrome surfaces. These triptychs form the centre of Deleuze's analysis.

Deleuze calls the rendering of the human body in Bacon's paintings the *Figure*. The Figure entertains a dynamic relation with the space around it but is at the same time isolated from this space by clear lines. The surrounding space itself is mostly empty, a monochrome surface emphasizing the contrast between the body and what surrounds it. According to Deleuze, sensations are not depicted or illustrated in these paintings, but embodied and enacted directly by the Figure. The paintings thus produce a non-representational rendering of sensation. Sensation is rendered through a movement that the Figure undergoes, but this movement is at the same time static. The Figure does not move to a different location but is the site of a movement. This movement takes place within the element of sensation. It is a movement or a *passage* from one sensation to another, from one intensity to another. It is an arrested movement, freezing the body in a particular contortion or typical position. A sense of gravity governing these Figures makes this arrested movement appear in the triptychs like a fall. The Figure is thus as if subjected to a gravitational pull, made to coincide affectively with its own body mass.

Aesthetically, this purification of the Figure involves a specific relationship between the line, the plane and the colour. The construction of a non-figurative visual space takes the form in Bacon's paintings of what Deleuze calls a *modular* relationship between line, plane and colour. Both the perspectival relations of figurative representation and the formal relations of abstract painting produce an *organized* visual space. Bacon, by contrast, establishes order by contrasting colours with one another. These relations of contrast are themselves purely chromatic, i.e. they are not organized by relations of light, but by the gradual contrasts between the colours in the chromatic spectrum. This modular chromatic space attains a kind of *flatness*, approaching two-dimensionality and the tactile quality of Egyptian relief painting. The negative task of avoiding figuration is thus fulfilled, positively, through the construction of a flat, chromatic, modular and *quasi-tactile* space where relations will not be programmed or coded by perspectival or formal relationships.

Deleuze thus describes Bacon's paintings as enacting a double movement of becoming. Psychological affects are becoming body, and the painting itself is taking on the plasticity of this embodied affect. Painting is thereby able to enact a becoming which is internal to the medium of painting but which is at the same time the becoming of a subject, a subject namely of becoming, a subject that is suspended in the static movement that it undergoes, a subject that exists only within this movement and which therefore remains unrepresentable, cut off from action and relationality. This subject of becoming is a subject of passivity, and Deleuze's ethics is an affirmation of passivity, a passivity expressed as a capacity to undergo affects and as the receptivity required to enter the movement of becoming.

The general theory of philosophy and the specialized studies on Leibniz, on cinema, and on Francis Bacon each trace a particular enactment and embodiment of thought within a sensory medium. In the case of philosophy, the medium is only virtually sensory in so far as philosophy is not identical with the textual or psychological media in which it manifests itself. Philosophy creates its own quasi-sensory medium, composed of the plane and the concepts that are constructed on the plane. Cinema is a directly sensory organization of light and movement, but it is also an interpretation of perception and its relation to action and time. Every film thereby makes a statement about the role of the human point of view within reality. The studies on Leibniz and Bacon interweave even more tightly the analysis of philosophical problems and the description of aesthetic structure, to the point where the fold (Leibniz) and the failing body (Bacon) are fully realized concrete embodiments of thought in a sensory or quasi-sensory space.

6

Conclusion: The Object of Philosophy

If we now at the end of this survey try to arrive at an overview of Deleuze's thought as a whole, both in its chronological development and in its diversity of themes, we can identify a number of strands running through his work and holding it together. Paradoxically, these unifying traits are not ideas or themes but consist of unresolved tensions and areas of problems that his thought struggles to master. In the collaborative work these problems give rise to some of Deleuze and Guattari's most innovative concepts. We can identify three such areas of problems. They all concern the nature of philosophy and the relationship between philosophy and reality, or, in other words, the object of philosophy.

In Deleuze's theory of philosophy, he formulates a version of the old logical concept of petition of principle, the notion that no system of thought can function without making assumptions that are not justified within the system. Deleuze calls these tacit assumptions, the 'plane' of a given philosophy. The most important feature of a plane is the assumptions it contains about reality, about what it means to be, about what kinds of things exist. The plane is correlated with a conception of the role of the philosopher.

Deleuze's own plane of philosophy is divided between two sharply distinct attitudes towards reality, each involving a different conception of human agency and the power of thought to influence reality. The first attitude is sceptical and contemplative. Reality is seen from this perspective as a composition of formal structuring principles, variously called 'ideas', 'stratifications', 'folds', etc. Human life, thought and agency exist within a reality constituted by these ideas, stratifications or folds. The life of an individual is then conditioned by a system of virtual points defining a destiny for that individual. The attitude of the philosopher towards reality is detached and fatalistic as he observes in the game of chance and repetition the cycle of civilizations replacing each other and endlessly repeating the conflict of states and nomads.

In opposition to this detached sceptical stance, Deleuze also occupies a passionate critical and ethical position. The philosophy of immanence is a strategy aimed at liberating both philosophy and life from the grip of 'representation', the subordination of our ability to think under the empirical framework of individual, identifiable objects and the subordination of life under the conscious application of moral rules.

In order to liberate our capacity for thought and potential for life, we have to dislodge the power of representation both within ourselves as moral-psychological beings and as philosophers. It is conceivable for us to do so because thoughts and affects embody an agency of a different kind from that of self-conscious subjectivity. This is the agency of the *'sujet larvaire'* and of 'becoming'. The ethics and epistemology of immanence realized as practice through the concepts of becoming and the embryonic subject entail a perspective on reality and on the agency of thought within reality that is opposed to the sceptical perspective of Deleuze's metaphysics.

The second area of tension that defines philosophy's relation to reality in his work is the tension between metaphysical and epistemological positions that are normally opposed, Leibnizian rationalism and Humean empiricism, a post-Kantian idealism (the virtual constitution of reality) and various forms of materialism. Some of these positions are held in succession: hence *Difference and Repetition* is more idealistic than *Anti-Oedipus*. However, there is a tension in Deleuze's metaphysics from beginning to end between a materialism that sees reality as arising out of a configuration of unformed matter and a quasi-mathematical idealism that sees reality as constituted by purely formal and abstract relationships.

Anti-Oedipus and *A Thousand Plateaus* present a semiotic solution to this conflict between materialism and idealism and use this semiotics to produce a non-empirical or non-representational theory of social reality.

Anti-Oedipus develops a theory of social categories. These categories are thought to be produced within the society in which they are valid in order to represent to the members of that society the essence and origin of that society. The categories have a dual ideal and material status. They are inscribed (*material process*) on a surface of sense (*ideal result*).

In *A Thousand Plateaus*, this method is applied within the context of a general theory of culture: all cultural practices, including all systems of thought and belief, come into being through a material process of idealization, or 'deterritorialization' whereby one process captures and formalizes the internal operating code of another, less abstract process.

This theory of culture as deterritorialized practice has implications also for Deleuze's conception of philosophy. According to *A Thousand Plateaus*, philosophy does not have a different role or status from that of natural and social sciences in that all thought is exercised within a social reality; all thought aspires to a genetic, or 'diagrammatic' understanding of reality, and all thought is exercised within a force field dominated by the dual pressures of transparent representation (*bi-univocity*) and non-representational thought (*rhizome*).

The third set of problems that runs through Deleuze's thought concerns the nature of this genetic understanding and the status of its 'objects'. Deleuze's early works on Hume, Bergson, Kant and Spinoza developed various conceptions of thought and immanence. Common to these was the assumption of a split between thought and object, between the immanent realm of thought and the objects that we identify in experience.

The development of an ontological system of virtual points, the social ontology of production (*Anti-Oedipus*) and stratification (*A Thousand Plateaus*) follow the same principle of immanence: virtualities, production, stratification are not given in experience. They are genetic principles that do not resemble objects that we can encounter within conscious experience.

This immanence of the objects of philosophical thought within philosophy itself moves Deleuze's thought close to Absolute Idealism. In the Absolute Idealism of Hegel, philosophy presents itself as a self-enclosed rational system that is supposed to account for reality as a whole in its ideal and intrinsic features. By contrast, Deleuze's genetic philosophy of difference does not conform to any such structural model. Nevertheless, the Deleuzian concept of immanence has an ambivalent relation to this kind of idealism: a self-sufficient system of reason is itself 'immanent' in the sense that reason is thought to justify itself within the system without having to rely on 'external' evidence taken from experience. Now, Deleuze's

principle of immanence differs from this self-sufficiency of a rational system in that it is *reality* and not the system that is thought to
constitute an order of immanence.

Such a concept of an immanent order presents an epistemological
problem about how philosophy may know this order. Deleuze
addresses this question through his theory of determination. The
genetic order of determination that constitutes the immanent order
of reality is not given to thought in the manner of an ideal structure.
In thought, we can only grasp this order of determination through
the problem, later the diagram, but we do not, as we would in a
philosophy of Absolute Idealism, have access to the complete system
of problems and diagrams.

The transition to aesthetics in Deleuze's last phase transforms
and formalizes the concept of immanence, shifting its application
from the ontological order of reality to the internal principles of
composition within philosophy and art. However, this shift continues the debate with philosophical idealism and rationalism: rationalistic philosophical systems are now reconstructed independently
of their own rational claims to self-justification. The immanence of
rationalism, whether in Plato, Leibniz or Hegel, consists in the claim
that philosophical reason is capable of absolute self-justification.
This is a pretension of philosophy that Deleuze has sought to criticize throughout his work. His constructivist theory of philosophy
gives a particular, aesthetic and formalist formulation of this criticism. According to this theory, philosophy can produce consistent
systems, but this systematicity is formal. It is the consistency of
concepts and their relations to a problem. It never amounts to a
structure of rational self-justification.

Notes

Introduction

1 All these thinkers can be termed 'cosmological metaphysicians'. They propose theories of the world or cosmos based on concepts of energy or force, such as the Stoic concept of fire, Spinoza's concept of divine nature, the system of 'monads' in Leibniz, Nietzsche's 'will to power', or Bergson's 'élan vital'. Deleuze interprets all of these thinkers as taking the view that mental activity is to be understood in relation to a cosmic field of forces of which it is a part.

2 Dorothea Olkowski, *Deleuze and the Ruin of Representation* (Berkeley, CA, 1999), p. 99.

3 I retain a direct translation of the French title instead of the less accurate English title, *Expressionism in Philosophy: Spinoza* (Cambridge, MA, 1992).

4 A prime example of this tradition is Martial Guéroult, *Descartes selon l'ordre des raisons* (Paris, 1953). Texts that directly influenced Deleuze include Martial Guéroult, *La Philosophie transcendantale de Salomon Maimon* (Paris, 1929); Victor Goldschmidt, *Le Système stoïcien et l'idée du temps* (Paris, 1969); and Jules Vuillémin, *L'Héritage kantien et la révolution copernicienne* (Paris, 1954).

5 Cf. the following review articles, of Régis Jolivet, 'Le problème de la mort chez M. Heidegger et J.-P. Sartre', *Revue philosophique de la France et de l'étranger* CXLIII(1–3) (janvier–mars 1953): 107–8; of K. E. Lögstrup, 'Kierkegaard und Heideggers Existenzanalyse und ihr Verhältnis zur Verkündigung', *Revue philosophique de la France et de l'étranger* CXLIII(1–3) (janvier–mars 1953): 108–9; and of Helmut Kuhn, 'Encounter with Nothingness/Begegnung mit dem Nichts', *Revue philosophique de la France et de l'étranger* CXLIII(1–3) (janvier–mars 1953): 109.

6 The view that these French philosophers were both radical critics of the concept of self-consciousness and that they were broadly hostile to the Enlightenment project has been argued by Luc Ferry and Alain Renaut, *La Pensée 68: essai sur l'anti-humanisme contemporain* (Paris, 1985).

7 The most orthodox practitioners of this semiotic programme were Algirdas Greimas and Tzvetan Todorov.

8 Cf. Gilles Deleuze, 'A quoi reconnaît-on le structuralisme?' in *L'Île déserte et autres texts* (Paris, 2002).

9 Georges Canguilhem, *Le Normal et le pathologique* (Paris, 1994); Georges Dumézil, *Les Dieux des indoeuropéens* (Paris, 1952).

10 This is the main theme of Deleuze's book *Nietzsche et la philosophie* (Paris, 1962).

11 Cf. Georges Bataille, *L'Expérience intérieure* (Paris, 1943).

12 Cf. Maurice Blanchot, *Le Livre à venir* (Paris, 1959), p. 42.

Chapter 1   Immanence and Subjectivity

1 Paul Guyer, 'Thought and being: Hegel's critique of Kant's theoretical philosophy', in Frederick C. Beiser (ed.), *The Cambridge Companion to Hegel* (Cambridge, 1993).

2 *Différence et répétition* (Paris, 1968), pp. 44–5, translation slightly modified from *Difference and Repetition* (London, 1994), p. 29.

3 *Différence et répétition* (Paris, 1968), p. 82, translation taken from *Difference and Repetition* (London, 1994), p. 59.

4 This necessary relationship between logic and perception is something that Aristotle takes for granted but Kant seeks to demonstrate in his *Critique of Pure Reason* ([London, 1781–7] Cambridge, 1998).

5 Plato, *Parmenides*, 130c, quoted from *Plato's Parmenides* (New Haven, CT, and London, 1997), p. 8, translation modified.

6 Heraclitus, from fragments 30 and 36, in G. S. Kirk, *Heraclitus: The Cosmic Fragments* (Cambridge, 1954), pp. 307, 339.

7 Gilles Deleuze, *La Philosophie critique de Kant: doctrine des facultés* (Paris, 1963), p. 25, quoted from the English translation, *Kant's Critical Philosophy: The Doctrine of the Faculties* (London, [1963] 1984), p. 15.

8 *Spinoza et le problème de l'expression* (Paris, 1968), p. 14, my translation.

9 Cf. Bernard Williams, *Descartes: The Project of Pure Enquiry* (London, 1990), p. 10.

10 Salomon Maimon, *Versuch über die Transzendentalphilosophie* (Berlin, 1790). On Maimon's philosophy, cf. Ernst Cassirer, *Das Erkenntnisproblem in der Philosophie und Wissenschaft der neueren Zeit* (Berlin, 1922–23). On his relation to Kant and Deleuze, cf. Juliette Simont, 'Essai sur la quantité, la qualité, la relation, chez Kant, Hegel, Deleuze', in *Les 'fleurs noires' de la logique philosophique* (Paris, 1997).

11 On the scientific background to Leibniz's metaphysics, cf. Ernst Cassirer, *Leibniz's System in seinen wissenschaftlichen Grundlagen* (Marburg, 1902).
12 Henri Bergson, *Creative Evolution* (London, [1908] 1960), p. xii.
13 *Différence et répétition* (Paris, 1968), p. 150, translation taken from *Difference and Repetition* (London, 1994), p. 114.
14 *Logique du sens* (Paris, 1968), p. 145, translation modified from *The Logic of Sense* (London, 1990), p. 120.
15 *Logique du sens* (Paris, 1968), p. 123, translation taken from *The Logic of Sense* (London, 1990), p. 101.
16 The fragment is from Sextus Empiricus. It is quoted in A. A. Long and D. N. Sedley, *The Hellenist Philosophers*, vols I–II (Cambridge, 1987), pp. 195–6.

Chapter 2 Cultural Semiotics

1 The first version of this essay appeared in 1964, but it was subsequently expanded and appeared in revised editions in 1970 and 1976, English translation, *Proust and Signs* (Minneapolis, 2000).
2 See Chapter 1, note 8.
3 There is an excellent introduction to Deleuze's reading of Proust in André Colombat, *Deleuze et la littérature* (New York, 1990).
4 The concept of the machine has its origin in Guattari's critique of the Lacanian concept of the subject, cf. Jean-Jacques Lecercle, *Deleuze and Language* (Basingstoke, 2002), pp. 180–1.
5 Joseph Conrad, *Heart of Darkness* (London, [1902] 1995), p. 35.

Chapter 3 A History of the Modern Subject

1 Eugene Holland, *Deleuze and Guattari's Anti-Oedipus: Introduction to Schizoanalysis* (London, 1999).
2 Immanuel Kant, *Kritik der reinen Vernunft* (Berlin [1781–7] 1922), English edition, *Critique of Pure Reason* (Cambridge, 1998), p. B 403.
3 Karl Marx, *The German Ideology*, student edn (London, [1846] 1970), p. 47.
4 Friedrich Nietzsche, *On the Genealogy of Morals* (Oxford, [1887] 1996), p. 65.
5 Sigmund Freud, *Three Essays on the Theory of Sexuality* (1905) in *The Standard Edition of the Complete Psychological Works of Sigmund Freud* (London, 1953), p. 180.
6 Marcel Mauss, *The Gift: The Form and Reason for Exchange in Archaic Societies* (London, [1950] 1990), p. 41.

7   Gilles Deleuze and Félix Guattari, *L'Anti-Oedipe, capitalisme et schizophré-nie*, vol. I (Paris, 1972), p. 281, this translation, slightly modified from *Anti-Oedipus* (London, 1984), p. 257.
8   *Anti-Oedipe*, p. 307; *Anti-Oedipus*, p. 280 (my translation).

Chapter 4   Social Ontology

1   Max Weber, *On Charisma and Institution Building: Selected Papers* (Chicago and London, 1968), p. 75.
2   Theodor W. Adorno, *Aesthetic Theory* (London, [1970] 1997).
3   Friedrich Nietzsche, *On the Genealogy of Morals* (Oxford, [1887] 1996), p. 64.
4   Theodor W. Adorno, 'Progress', in Rolf Tiedemann (ed.), *Can One Live after Auschwitz? A Philosophical Reader* (Stanford, CA, 2003), p. 127.
5   John Rajchman, *The Deleuze Connections* (Cambridge, MA, 2000), p. 8.
6   Raymond Aron, *Main Currents in Sociological Thought*, vol. 2 (London, 1967), p. 15. Durkheim conceived of social reality as an autonomous realm, composed of collective representations that exist independently of individuals, but at the same time he understood these representations as factors shaping idividual beliefs and actions.
7   John Plamenatz, *Man and Society*, vol. II (Harlow, 1963), p. 37.
8   Gilles Deleuze and Félix Guattari, *Mille Plateaux: capitalisme et schizophrénie*, vol. II (Paris, 1980), p. 146, this translation slightly modified from *A Thousand Plateaus* (London, 1988), p. 116.

Chapter 5   Philosophy and Art

1   English translation (Minneapolis, 1993).
2   *The Fold: Leibniz and the Baroque* (London, 1993), p. 45.

Bibliography

Bibliographical Survey of Works on Deleuze

A large number of books devoted either to Deleuze or to Deleuze and Guattari have appeared during the past decade in the English-speaking world. Some of these works are introductory, others are more specialized. Important works have also appeared in French, Italian and German. The following survey presents some of these texts, grouping them thematically as well as indicating their level of difficulty.

I said in the Introduction that commentators take different views on a number of very basic issues in the interpretation of Deleuze's philosophy (both his own and the philosophy developed with Guattari), in particular: (1) the relationship between his philosophy and the metaphysical tradition beginning with Plato; and (2) the view that this philosophy presents on human thought and action.

Four of the most significant commentators on Deleuze are Véronique Bergen, Dorothea Olkowski, Alain Badiou and John Rajchman. They take different views on these issues and in particular they take different views on Deleuze's conception of philosophical thought.

In *La Clameur de l'être* (1997), Badiou presents a purely metaphysical reading of Deleuze. He emphasizes the cosmological perspective on human life in Deleuze's thought and argues that there are formal similarities between his philosophy of difference and the neo-Platonic ontology of the One beyond being. Badiou thereby implies that thinking would aspire to some kind of metaphysical truth. This view does not take into account the novelty of Deleuze's account of thought as a creative process. The commentaries by Bergen, Olkowski and Rajchman, by contrast, do exactly that.

Bergen's *L'Ontologie de Gilles Deleuze* (2001) thus analyses the theme of creation in Deleuze, a theme that she locates both on the level of 'being' and within thought itself. Being and thought thereby appear as parallel creative processes that cannot be mapped within the traditional philosophical vocabulary of 'representation'.

This so-called 'representational' model of thought is also the topic of Olkowski's *Deleuze and the Ruin of Representation*. She opposes *representation*, which she sees as a universal and homogenous thought-form, to a conception of mental activity as a process that is grounded in habit and irreducible to any general, representational thought form.

John Rajchman in his *The Deleuze Connections* (2000) is attentive to the novelty of Deleuze's own method of *doing* philosophy – his modernity both as a thinker and as a writer. Rather than reconstructing Deleuze's system, Rajchman's book therefore re-enacts the thought processes that take place within Deleuze's philosophy.

Of these four commentaries, those written by Badiou, Rajchman and Olkowski are very clear and accessible whereas Véronique Bergen's book demands a more dedicated reader.

Apart from these four books offering substantial interpretations of Deleuze's thought as a whole, there are a number of introductory essays worth mentioning. Todd May's *Gilles Deleuze: An Introduction* (2005) focuses on the ontological concepts of difference and individuation. A study of Deleuze's philosophy of difference with a stronger emphasis on the theories developed in *The Logic of Sense* is that of G. Battista Vaccaro, *Deleuze e il pensiero del molteplice* (1990). François Zoubarchivili's *La philosophie de l'événement* (1994) provides a good survey of Deleuze's theories of force and time. Another study that explains these concepts, but with an original focus on Deleuze's early historical works on Hume, Nietzsche and Spinoza, is Michael Hardt's *Gilles Deleuze: An Apprenticeship in Philosophy* (1993).

Apart from these interpretative introductions, there are a number of texts that are introductory in a different sense. They provide clear and concise summaries of different areas and themes in Deleuze's philosophy. In this category are the books by Paul Patton, *Deleuze and the Political* (2000), Claire Colebrook, *Understanding Deleuze* (2002) and Ronald Bogue's two books, *Deleuze on Literature* (2003a) and *Deleuze on Painting, Music and the Arts* (2003b).

There are also a number of texts which lie between summary and interpretation and which are devoted to a quite specific text or area of problems. In this category I would especially recommend Jean-Jacques Lecercle, *Deleuze and Language* (2002). It presents Deleuze's various semiotic models and discusses their relevance for literary studies. Another inspiring book written a few years back is Brian Massumi's *A User's Guide to Capitalism and Schizophrenia* (1992) which presents a political and ontological reading of *A Thousand Plateaus*. David Norman Rodowick's *Gilles Deleuze's Time Machine* (1997) situates Deleuze's philosophy of cinema within international film studies, while James Williams' *Gilles Deleuze's 'Difference and Repetition': A Critical Introduction and Guide* (2003) is an engaging critical dialogue with *Difference and Repetition*. Manuel Delanda's *Intensive Science and Virtual Philosophy* (2002) shows the compatibility between Deleuze's ontology and contemporary science while Marc Rödli's *Philosophie des transzendentalen Empirismus* (2003) analyses Deleuze's account of perception in *Difference and Repetition* within the context of an underlying debate between Humean empiricism, Kantian transcendental philosophy and Husserlian phenomenology.

There are also a number of stimulating collections of essays on Deleuze. Among them I would like to highlight in particular Jean Khalfa (ed.), *Introduction to the Philosophy of Gilles Deleuze* (2003), Constantin Bundas and Dorothea Olkowski (eds), *Gilles Deleuze and the Theatre of Philosophy* (1994), Pierre Verstreten and Isabelle Stengers, *Gilles Deleuze* (1998) and the bilingual, French and German volume *Der Film bei Deleuze/Le cinéma selon Deleuze*, edited by Oliver Fahle and Lorenz Engel (1998).

Sometimes people ask which of Deleuze's books one should begin with – but there is no correct answer to this. One can start with the introductions Deleuze himself gave to his philosophy, the *Dialogues* with Claire Parnet (1987) and the interviews collected in *Negotiations*. Or one can start with one of his early works devoted to an individual thinker or writer. Or one can begin with one of the large treatises *Anti-Oedipus* or *The Movement-Image*.

Selected Works by Gilles Deleuze

Empirisme et Subjectivité (Paris, 1953) [*Empiricism and Subjectivity*, New York, Oxford, 1991].
Nietzsche et la philosophie (Paris, 1962) [*Nietzsche and Philosophy*, London, 1983].

La Philosophie critique de Kant (Paris, 1963) [*Kant's Critical Philosophy*, London, 1983].

Marcel Proust et les signes (Paris, 1964) [*Proust and Signs*, London, 2000].

Le Bergsonisme (Paris, 1966) [*Bergsonism*, New York, 1988].

Présentation de Sacher Masoch (Paris, 1967) [*Masochism*, New York, 1989].

Différence et répétition (Paris, 1968) [*Difference and Repetition*, London, 1994].

Spinoza et la problème de l'expression (Paris, 1968) [*Expressionism in Philosophy: Spinoza*, New York, 1990].

Logique du sens (Paris, 1968) [*The Logic of Sense*, London, 1990].

Spinoza: Philosophie pratique (Paris, 1970) [*Spinoza: Practical Philosophy*, San Francisco, 1988].

Francis Bacon: Logique de la sensation (Paris, 1981).

Cinéma I, L'Image-mouvement (Paris, 1983) [*Cinema 1: The Movement-Image*, London, 1992].

Cinéma II, L'image-temps (Paris, 1985) [*Cinema 2: The Time-Image*, London, 1989].

Foucault (Paris, 1986) [*Foucault*, London, 1988].

Le Pli: Leibniz et le baroque (Paris, 1988) [*The Fold: Leibniz and the Baroque*, London, 1993].

Pour-parlers 1972–1990 (Paris, 1990) [*Negotiations*, New York, 1995].

Critique et clinique (Paris, 1993) [*Essays Critical and Clinical*, Minneapolis, 1997].

With Félix Guattari

L'Anti-Oedipe: Capitalisme et schizophrénie I (Paris, 1972) [*Anti-Oedipus*, London, 1984].

Kafka: Pour une litérature mineure (Paris, 1975) [*Kafka: Toward a Minor Literature*, Minneapolis, 1986].

Mille Plateaux: Capitalisme et schizophrénie II (Paris, 1980) [*A Thousand Plateaus*, London, 1988].

Qu'est-ce que la philosophie? (Paris, 1991) [*What Is Philosophy?*, New York, 1994].

With Claire Parnet

Dialogues (Paris, 1977) [*Dialogues*, London, 1987].

Early Review Articles

Review of Régis Jolivet, 'Le problème de la mort chez M. Heidegger et J.-P. Sartre', *Revue philosophique de la France et de l'étranger* CXLIII(1–3) (janvier–mars 1953): 107–8; of K. E. Lögstrup, 'Kierkegaard und Heideggers Existenzanalyse und ihr Verhältnis zur Verkündigung', *Revue philosophique de la France et de l'étranger* CXLIII(1–3) (janvier–mars 1953): 108–9, and of Helmut Kuhn, 'Encounter with Nothingness/Begegnung mit dem Nichts', *Revue philosophique de la France et de l'étranger* CXLIII(1–3) (janvier–mars 1953): 109.

Lectures

Some of Deleuze's lectures from the University of Vincennes are on the Web at www.webdeleuze.com.

Posthumous Collections of Articles

L'Île deserte et autres textes: Textes et entretiens, 1952–1974, ed. David Lapoujade (Paris, 2002).
Deux régimes de fous: Textes et entretiens, 1975–1995, ed. David Lapoujade (Paris, 2003).

Works by Other Authors

Adorno, Theodor W., *Aesthetic Theory* (London, 1997).
——*Can One Live after Auschwitz?* (Stanford, CA, 2003).
Aristotle, *Metaphysics*, trans. H. G. Apostle (Bloomington, IN, and London, 1966).
——*Le Catégorie*, trans. M. Zanatta (Milan, 1989).
Aron, Raymond, *Main Currents in Sociological Thought*, vol. 2 (London, 1967).
Artaud, Antonin, *Œuvres Complètes*, vol. I (Paris, 1970).
Aubenque, Pierre, *Le Problème de l'être chez Aristotle: Essai sur la problématique aristotélicienne* (Paris, 1962).
Badiou, Alain, *Deleuze: La Clameur de l'être*, Paris, 1997, translated as *The Clamor of Being* (Minneapolis, 2000).
Bataille, Georges, *L'Expérience intérieure* (Paris, 1943).

——*La part maudite* (Paris, 1967).

Bergen, Véronique, *L'Ontologie de Gilles Deleuze* (Paris, 2001).

Bergson, Henri, *Creative Evolution* (London, 1960).

Blanchot, Maurice, *L'Espace littéraire* (Paris, 1955).

——*Le livre à venir* (Paris, 1959).

Bogue, Ronald, *Deleuze on Literature* (London, 2003a).

——*Deleuze on Painting, Music and the Arts* (London, 2003b).

Brehier, Emile, *La Théorie des incorporéels dans l'ancien stoïcisme* (Paris, 1928).

Bundas, Constantin V., 'Deleuze and subject-formation', in Constantin V. Bundas and Dorothea Olkowski (eds) *Gilles Deleuze and the Theatre of Philosophy* (New York and London, 1994).

Bundas, Constantin V. and Olkowski, Dorothea (eds) *Gilles Deleuze and the Theatre of Philosophy* (New York and London, 1994).

Canetti, Elias, *Der andere Prozess* (München, 1969).

Canguilhem, Georges, *Le Normal et le pathologique* (Paris, 1994).

Cassirer, Ernst, *Leibniz's System in seinen wissenschaftlichen Grundlagen* (Marburg, 1902).

——*Das Erkenntnisproblem in der Philosophie und Wissenschaft der neueren Zeit* (Berlin, 1922–23).

Colebrook, Claire, *Understanding Deleuze* (Crow's Nest, 2002).

Colombat, André, *Deleuze et la littérature* (New York, 1990).

Delanda, Mauel, *Intensive Science and Virtual Philosophy* (London, 2002).

Descartes, René, *Œuvres et lettres* (Paris, 1970).

D'Or, Joël, *Introduction à la lecture de Lacan* (Paris, 2002).

Dosse, François, *Histoire du structuralisme*, vols I–II (Paris, 1991–92).

Dumézil, Georges, *Les Dieux des indoeuropéens* (Paris, 1952).

Durkheim, Emile, *The Division of Labour in Society* (New York, [1893] 1933).

Fahle, Oliver and Engel, Lorenz (eds), *Der Film bei Deleuze/Le cinéma selon Deleuze* (Paris, 1998).

Foucault, Michel, 'Les mots et les choses' (Paris, 1966).

——*L'Archéologie du savoir* (Paris, 1969).

——*Surveiller et punir* (Paris, 1975).

Freud, Sigmund, *Three Essays on the Theory of Sexuality*, in *The Standard Edition of the Complete Psychological Works of Sigmund Freud* (London, [1905] 1953).

——*Gesammelte Werke* (Frankfurt am Main, 1999).

Gerson, Lloyd P., *Plotinus* (London, 1994).

Goethe, Johann Wolfgang von, *Werke*, vol. III, *Dramatische Dichtungen, erster Band,* (Hamburg, 1949).

Goldschmidt, Victor, *Le Système stoïcien et l'idée du temps* (Paris, 1969).

Gombrowicz, Witold, *Ferdydurke* (London, 1965).

Guéroult, Martial, *La Philosophie transzendantale de Salomon Maimon* (Paris, 1929).

——*Descartes selon l'ordre des raisons* (Paris, 1953).

Guyer, Paul, 'Thought and being: Hegel's critique of Kant's theoretical philosophy', in Frederick C. Beiser (ed.), *The Cambridge Companion to Hegel* (Cambridge, 1993).

Hankinson, R. J., *Cause and Explanation in Ancient Greek Thought* (Oxford, 1998).

Hardt, Michael, *An Apprenticeship in Philosophy* (London, 1993).

Hegel, G. W. *Wissenschaft der Logik*, vols I–III (Hamburg, 1978–).

Heidegger, Martin, *Sein und Zeit* (Tübingen, 1927).

Hjelmslev, Louis, *Prolegomena to a Theory of Language* (Madison, WI, [1943] 1963).

Hobbes, Thomas, *Leviathan* (Indianapolis, [1651] 1994).

Holland, Eugene, *Deleuze and Guattari's Anti-Oedipus: Introduction to Schizoanalysis* (London, 1999).

Honnefelder, Ludger, *Ens Inquantum Ens, Der Begriff des Seienden als solchen als Gegenstand der Metaphysik nach der Lehre des Johannes Duns Scotus* (Münster, 1979).

Husserl, Edmund, *Ideen zu einer reinen Phänomenologie und phänomenologischen Philosophie* (HAAG, 1950–52).

Kafka, Franz, *Erzählungen* (Berlin, 1935).

Kant, Immanuel, *Kritik der reinen Vernunft* (Berlin, [1787] 1922).

——*Critique of Pure Reason* (Cambridge, 1998).

Khalfa, Jean, *An Introduction to the Philosophy of Gilles Deleuze* (London, 2003).

Klossowski, Pierre, *Le Baphomet* (Paris, 1965).

Kroner, Richard, *Von Kant bis Hegel* (Tübingen, 1921–24).

Lacan, Jacques, *Ecrits* (Paris, 1966).

——*Le Séminaire de Jacques Lacan, Livre 1, Les écrits techniques de Freud, 1953–54* (Paris, 1975).

——*Le Séminaire de Jacques Lacan, Livre 2, Le moi dans la théorie de Freud et dansla technique de la psychanalyse, 1954–1955* (Paris, 1980).

Lecercle, Jean-Jacques, *Deleuze and Language* (Basingstoke, 2002).

Leibniz, G. W., *Die philosophische Schriften*, vols I–VII, ed. C. I. Gerhardt (Berlin, 1875, 1890).

Lévi-Strauss, Claude, *Les Structures eléméntaires de la parenté* (Berlin, [1947] 2002).

Long, A. A. and Sedley, D. N., *The Hellenistic Philosophers*, vols I–II (Cambridge, 1987).

Macherey, Pierre, *Hegel ou Spinoza* (Paris, 1979).

Maimon, Salomon, *Versuch über die Transzendentalphilosophie* (Berlin, 1790).

Martinez, Francisco José, *Ontologia y diferencia: La filosofia de Gilles Deleuze* (Madrid, 1987).

Marx, Karl, *Werke, Schriften, Briefe*, 6 vols (Stuttgart, 1966–71).

—— *The German Ideology*, Students edn, (London, [1846] 1970).

Massumi, Brian, *A User's Guide to Capitalism and Schizophrenia: Deviations from Deleuze and Guattari* (Cambridge, MA, 1992).

Mauss, Marcel, *The Gift: The Form and Reason of Exchange in Archaic Societies*, (London, [1950] 1990).

May, Todd, *Gilles Deleuze: An Introduction* (Cambridge, 2005).

Musil, Robert, *Der Mann ohne Eigenschaften*, in *Gesammelte Werke*, vols I–V, (Hamburg, 1978).

Nietzsche, F. R., *Sämtliche Werke: kritische Studienausgabe in 15 Einzelbanden* (Munchen, 1988).

—— *On the Genealogy of Morals* (Oxford, [1887] 1996).

Olkowski, Dorothea, *Deleuze and the Ruin of Representation* (Berkeley, CA, 1999).

Pardo, José Luis, 'De quatre formules poétiques qui pourraient résumer la philosophie deleuzienne', in Pierre Verstreten and Isabelle Stengers (eds), *Gilles Deleuze* (Paris, 1998).

Patton, Paul, *Deleuze and the Political* (London, 2000).

Philippe, Jonathan, 'Nietzsche and Spinoza: new personae in a new plane of thought', in Jean Khalfa, *Introduction to the Philosophy of Gilles Deleuze* (London, 2003).

Plamenatz, John, *Man and Society*, vol. II (Harlow, 1963).

Plato, *Phaedo* (London, 1955).

—— *Parmenides* (New Haven, CT, and London, 1997).

Proust, Marcel, *A la recherche du temps perdu*, vols I–III (Paris, 1954).

Rajchman, John, *The Deleuze Connections* (Cambridge, MA, 2000).

Robbe-Grillet, Alain, *Les Gommes* (Paris, 1953).

Rödli, Marc, *Philosophie des transzendentalen Empirismus* (Vienna, 2003).

Rodowick, David Norman, *Gilles Deleuze's Time Machine* (Durham, NC, 1997).

Rosen, Stanley, *The Question of Being: A Reversal of Heidegger* (New Haven, CT, 1993).

Safouan, Moustafa, *Lacaniana: Les séminaires de 1953–1963* (Paris, 2001).

Saussure, Ferdinand de, *Cours de linguistique générale* (Paris, 1995).

Simont, Juliette, 'Essai sur la quantité, la qualité, la relation, chez Kant, Hegel, Deleuze', in *Les 'fleurs noires' de la logique philosophique* (Paris, 1997).

—— 'Intensity or: the "Encounter"', in Jean Khalfa, *An Introduction to the Philosophy of Gilles Deleuze* (London, 2003).

Sokolowski, Robert, *The Formation of Husserl's Concept of Constitution* (The Hague, 1964).

Spinoza, Benedictus de, *Œuvres*, vols I–III, trans. Appuhn (Paris, 1929).

Vaccaro, G. Battista, *Deleuze e il pensiero del molteplice* (Milan, 1990).

Verstreten, Pierre and Stengers, Isabelle, *Gilles Deleuze* (Paris, 1998).

Vuillémin, Jules, *L'Héritage kantien et la révolution copernicienne* (Paris, 1954).

Weber, Max, *On Charisma and Institution Building* (Chicago, 1968).

—— *Economy and Society: An Outline of Interpretive Sociology* (Berkeley, CA, 1978).

Williams, Bernard, *Descartes: The Project of Pure Enquiry* (London, 1990).

Williams, James, *Gilles Deleuze's 'Difference and Repetition': A Critical Introduction and Guide* (Edinburgh, 2003).

Wittfogel, Karl A., *Oriental Despotism: A Comparative Study of Total Power* (New Haven, CT, 1957).

Zarader, Marlène, *L'Être et le neutre: A partir de Maurice Blanchot* (Lagrasse, 2001).

Zechner, Ingo, *Deleuze: Der Gesang des Werdens* (München, 2003).

Zourabichivili, François, *Deleuze: Une philosophie de l'événement* (Paris, 1994).

Index

The index is intended as a guide to the main themes of the book and to the most important technical terms used by Deleuze and Guattari.

Lightning Source UK Ltd.
Milton Keynes UK
UKOW030817221111

182425UK00001B/130/P